TO KAT,

*GOOD L
  LOVE,
HORSES LIKE MYSELF.*

Harry Wooding

Liverpool's Working Horses

by
Harry Wooding

Print Origination (NW) Limited
Formby
Liverpool L37 8EG

My grateful thanks to James and Lynne for their encouragement during the writing of this book

© Harry Wooding 1991

ISBN 903348 23 3

REPRINTED 2002

The author expresses his thanks to The E. Chambre Hardman Trust for their kind permission to reproduce photographs.

Typesetting by Print Origination (NW) Ltd., Formby Liverpool L37 8EG
Printed and bound in Great Britain by The Cromwell Press, Wiltshire.

Contents

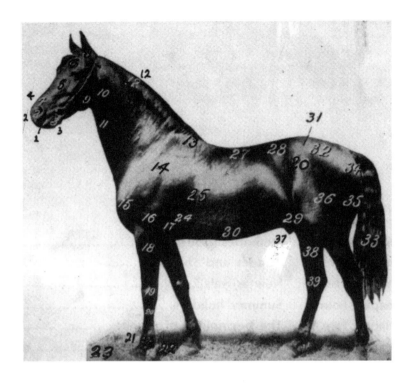

Points of the horse.

1. Mouth.	14. Shoulder.	27. Back.
2. Nostril.	15. Breast.	28. Loin.
3. Chin.	16. Arm.	29. Rear flank.
4. Nose.	17. Elbow.	30. Belly.
5. Face.	18. Forearm.	31. Hip.
6. Forehead.	19. Knee.	32. Croup.
7. Eye.	20. Cannon.	33. Tail.
8. Ear.	21. Fetlock.	34. Buttock.
9. Lower jaw.	22. Pastern.	35. Quarters.
10. Throatlatch.	23. Foot.	36. Thigh.
11. Windpipe.	24. Fore flank.	37. Stifle.
12. Crest.	25. Heart girth.	38. Lower thigh.
13. Withers.	26. Coupling.	39. Hock.

Chapter One,

Memories
1930's 1940's

I was born into a large family of four boys and five girls. Our home in Telford Street, Edge Hill was quite big by 1930 standards. Telford Street itself was quite small having only five houses on one side and our house and stables only on the opposite side; at the top of the street on our side, stood a public bakehouse.

The house we lived in, seemed to me, as a small boy, to have lots of rooms; three large bedrooms, two large parlours, two kitchens and what we called Cooeeys, which meant a passage way that led to nowhere, which were rather scarey as they had no light in them. It was railway property and built on top of a tunnel. At the bottom of our yard was the railway wall with a 60 foot drop on to the railway lines behind it.

Most of us children attended a quaint little church school at the highest part of Edge Hill, it was named St Marys; a Church of England school. It's classrooms were very tiny and were lit by gas mantles during dark winter afternoons.

Most of the teachers spent their entire working life at one school in those days, having taught mother then daughter or father and then son, so they almost knew your pedigree and what kind of family background you had. The teachers were very strict but fair, and all children were in awe of them. It was unheard of to question a teacher's motives or answer back. There was no graffiti

1

or violence in the playground and even the school caretaker was held in the greatest respect, as he knew all your families and if you did not behave according to his rules, which were; no cheeking the teacher; no running around the toilets; no swear words; even no talking on the stairs or behaving in a silly fashion. He would administer punishment himself, which seems hard by today's standards you may think, but it was best for a happy school.

My father worked for the Liverpool Health Committee, which went under the heading of L.H.C. He was a horse carter and the stable he was attached to, was in Smithdown Lane, about 10 minutes walk away from where we lived.

The stables were always alive with the hustle and bustle of the working day, which meant the comings and goings of carters with their great shire horses going about their daily tasks. There were a great variety of daily jobs as everything was done by horse carting in the 1930's. One of the jobs being done by pony and trap was the collecting and delivering of mail from the Municipal Buildings in Dale Street to all corporation depots, parks and gardens and cemeteries. Each of three main yards had its own pony and trap, Smithdown Lane, Gascoyne Street and Laverock Bank. The ponies did their journeys twice a day. Gascoyne Street serviced all northern depots with mail, Smithdown Lane all central, Laverock Bank all southern districts, so the ponies had to work hard, sometimes travelling 20 to 25 miles daily, always at the trot.

It was so interesting for me as a young boy because horses filled my world.

Because my father was so well respected, I was given the privilege of being allowed to call at the yard each day after finishing school at 4 o'clock. I would race down to the stables and because I was never afraid of the big shire horses, I was allowed to exercise the sick or lame horses whilst waiting for my father to arrive back at the depot with his great horse named Delightful. Every horse had a number and Delightful was 153.

The Head Horse Keeper was a Mr Tom Lee, who lived in the big

2

house inside the stable yard. Mr and Mrs Lee allowed me many privileges and seemed fond of me, I suppose because they had no children of their own.

At the top of the yard there was a huge cookhouse with a large fire going night and day, even on Sundays. At the side of the fire was a huge black kettle with a brass polished tap, which was always boiling so carters could brew their tea up at any time, and if they had not had any breakfast at home, they could cook egg and bacon on large baking tins. What a treat to have a large bacon butty and dip, and a lid of tea, pure heaven on a wet winters day.

A fine specimen of a Railway Clydesdale in gears

Old Spud Gaskell was the night man. He started work at 7pm and worked until 7am every day, Sundays included. He would see to the cookhouse fire and build it up for the night, fill the large kettle which held about ten gallons, then set about mixing the feeds for the horses for the next day. There were about seventy horses and ponies to feed and this all had to be done before 5am so that the horses would have had their morning feed before the carters arrived. As the carters came in, they would have to clock on by the huge clock which stood outside the cookhouse. Each

3

man had a numbered key which he inserted into the clock which recorded the time he clocked in or out. Each carter would then read his orders from a large worksheet inside the cookhouse. This sheet would explain everything you needed to know, such as the number of the horse you would be working, whether you were working a container or float, a team wagon or the street cleaning brush wagon. There were also other vehicles for carrying paving stones, sand and gravel or tar vats for repairing the roads. There was every kind of horse drawn wagon you could name, all of which had their own number, just like the horses.

Most regular carters had their own horses every day, except the days when the horse was sick or needed shoeing, then you would have to work a spare horse. Each horses name and number appeared on the worksheet and you could tell by the number what the age was and how long it had been in service. That applied to every horse in every stable in depots all over Liverpool.

Every horse stables had a Horsekeeper in charge and these days when I pass the silent buildings, I get a lump in my throat and remember former Horsekeepers, such as Mr George Roberts at the lodge in Smithdown Road, Mr Gandy at Gascoyne Street, Mr Boswell at Green Lane. There were many more, but you can guess Smithdown Lane was my favourite. I was always there when not at school and my mother never worried if I wasn't home from school, she knew where I would be as my love of the horses was so great.

Mr Lee would be in the office by the gate with young Charlie the Clerk. I would walk straight into the yard which no unauthorised person could do, so I was conscious of the honour. Mr Lee would come out of the office and say 'Hello Harry, would you like to exercise *Kafir* (160) or *Jason* or *Idol*' just three of the horses that had been laid off sick that week, but still needed light exercise around the yard, 'or would you like to give Tom Taylor (the day man) a hand to help prepare the feeds for the horses evening meal.'

Sometimes on a Monday he would ask me to run a little errand for him, such as going down to Grove Street to change his accumulator for his old radio set which was exchanged weekly otherwise there was no power in the radio. When I brought the accumulator back I was always sure of a large slice of cake off Mrs Lee. There was always something to keep me busy before the horses returned from their daily tasks like mixing provender, boiling beans and oats mixing in treacle, which I often spread on a slice of dry bread, no wonder the horses looked forward to it, it tastes lovely!

Portrait of two good friends

Photo E. Chambre Hardman F.R.P.S.   *Courtesy of the E. Chambre Hardman Trust.*

I would go into the massive lofts which to me was like entering another world. Huge machines used for cutting the hay into chop, stacks of oats in large sacks, also barley and beans all ready to be crushed for the horses feeds. Bales of straw stacked high to the ceiling for the horses' bedding. One of my little tasks each day was to drop a couple of bales down a hatch to the stalls below. I didn't realise until much later why I was allowed to do this job; because it meant climbing many stairs and walking right along the loft to truck the bales of straw to the hatch where you dropped them down. As the men had been climbing the stairs all day, they were quite happy to let me do it for them, seeing as I was so eager. No matter what job they gave me, I loved it because it allowed me to wander anywhere in the stables without being questioned and I felt I belonged there. I could even go into the huge attic around the back of the stables where all the show leathers and brasses were kept. It was like Aladdin's cave. It was only opened up once a year when the many parades and shows were on. Even men who had worked there years never saw the inside of this room, it was Mr Lee's *Holy of Holys*.

I knew where everything was kept. One of the jobs on Saturday mornings was to cut up the large blocks of soap into pieces, so each carter could take a piece to wash his horses legs and scrub all collars and under saddles which were made of canvas. If a horse had more than one white fetlock, or if it was a grey horse, he would take at least two pieces of soap.

Some men had black *gears*[2] which had to be varnished so I would fill up all the varnish tins and put the brushes by them for the men to pick up if they needed them, but most of the carters had what were called *Bright Gears,*[1] *so they would get a tin of Brasso*[18] to make the chains come up sparkling (hence the name *Brights*[1]). All the carters were allowed a supply of blacking which was scooped from a seven pound tin; the supply was kept in their pockets for cleaning when they had a few minutes to spare during their lunch hour.

Saturday was a hive of activity, as each horse returned from his days work anytime between 11.30am to 3pm. They were all given a Saturday treat a bucket of bran mash which was steaming hot, the horses always knew it was Saturday.

6

Show horses in competitons

When they had finished their meal, they would then be washed and groomed and bedded down on clean straw. All their gears would be polished and sparkling, then everything was tidied up. All the drinking buckets would be put under the taps ready for the next day, spades, *pikles*[3] and brushes were all lined up like soldiers, then all the remaining parts of the stables were sprinkled with white sawdust. It looked a real picture when you had your last look around before going home on your half day, not one thing was ever left out of place.

Sunday was always a special day at the stables. Every carter would be on rota to do a Sunday turn on duty, your turn came about every sixth Sunday. When it was my father's turn, he would come into the bedroom at about 5am to give me a shake. Although I was tired only being a small boy, he always knew how upset I would be if he had gone without me. We would just get a wash and have nothing to eat or drink, knowing that my mother would have left bacon and eggs and tea and sugar to take with us for us to cook on the big fire that would be waiting to greet us. There would be about six carters arriving, each one allocated a certain number of horses to water and muck out. My father always made sure that we would do our horses around 'the back' as he called it, where there were about twenty loose boxes and our great friend *Delightful* occupied Box No 3. It would be about 10.30am before the work was completed. All the men would have a final lid of tea, clock off and then go home. Some men had push bikes, but we were lucky, we only had to walk up Grinfield Street, down Harbourd Street to our house in Telford Street. At 3.30pm again, the men would repeat the same duties and leave the horses happy and the stables spotless and ready for Monday morning.

Author as a small boy (bottom left) with a large friend.

Chapter Two

Parades and Shows

In those days there were always lots of horse shows and parades in which you could enter. This was a great time for carters to try and outshine each other. There were different classes to be entered; the neatest and cleanest horse and gears; best team of horses; and the best decorated. Each year the men who were entering would be thinking up different ideas to decorate their horses. This was always a closely guarded secret until a day or two before the showing. Perhaps there had been a special national event and this theme was used.

On the May Day parades, nearly all local firms would enter, also the railways and corporation horses. Firms such as Larry Marr; Jarvis Robinson; Geo. Davies; William Harper; Garlick Burrell & Edwards; The Liverpool Cartage Co; Hobbs & Clark; Pelling Stanley; and A.V. Crutchley. Many a coal man with just one good horse would fancy his chance, even the old milk horse and bread delivery horse, all had their day of glory like beauty queens. All the horses would make their way to Abercromby Square which was an ideal place for judging the turn outs. Some of these teams would be pulling great loads of goods of every description, logs from West Africa, tobacco, sugar and ground nuts to name just a few, but still the carters brushed and cleaned them and kept them up to standard, as men would judge each other by the state of his horse during working hours.

My father with *Delightful* in full splendour ready for a show
(with me running in the background)

Many of the great carters names crop up from time to time even today, the likes of Billy Hall, Joe Thornton, Dick Benson, and the one who I thought was the best of all, my dad George Wooding.

It was not only my father who was involved in preparing *Delightful* for the May Day parades and shows, all the family were involved, my sisters had their own tasks to perform. Each evening after our meal was finished and everything washed up and cleared away, on to the big kitchen table came all the beautiful silks and ribbons which had to be stitched and fringed into the different shapes to decorate the *bridle*,[7] *collar*[17] and *breeching*[16] My brothers also had their little tasks to do. My father would only trust them to do the small buckles and straps. My elder brothers would be trusted to do the bigger jobs, such as linking the *brights*[1], for example. Chains, *ridgeworth*[13] and *crank*[12] and the *hames*[8] these all shone like silver when they were cleaned. My father would do all of the leather work as he was a great polisher of leather. He even made his own special blacking, although how he made it was always a secret. He always carried a tin of it in his working jacket and a large washed beef cloth which my mother would obtain from Mr Broad the local butcher in Wavertree Road. They were marvellous cloths which were used as coverings on lamb carcases, but after mother had boiled and washed them sparkling white, they were nice and soft and large enough to cover the cleaned gears and newly made flowers until show day. This cleaning of the gears was done every evening for at least two weeks before a show.

My mother had her work cut out while all this was going on. You can just imagine what her front parlour was like with all kinds of horse gears and chains and newly made flowers and brass bells tinkling away every time she tried to dust the room, but oh the joy and excitement which ran through the whole family when the great day dawned and they were all placed on *Delightful's* huge beautiful frame.

The day of the show would find the stable yards alive with activity. The horses going to the show were fed about 4am, old Spud Gaskell had seen to that. My father and I, and most of the carters who were showing, had been there all night. After all the washing and grooming you had to make sure the horses didn't lie down

11

again and get stained, undoing all the hard work especially the grey horses.

My dad would cook our eggs and bacon on the large fire in the cookhouse, whilst I toasted thick slices of bread with a long handled toasting fork, which had seen many years of service. Even the big, black kettle seemed to know it was a special day and the big stone olley⁴ inside seemed to rattle all the louder, it must have witnessed this scene many times over the years.

The men would then all brew up carefully taking their parcels of tea, sugar and condensed milk which was usually made up in a piece of the previous evenings echo. It made a smashing brew, you couldn't beat it. Every man had his own tea can and lid, which no-one else used.

Now came the hour to start seriously on the horses. All had to be groomed once more for at least an hour. Their manes and tails had to be brushed and combed out ready for plaiting with the coloured raffia and ribbons, then there followed about 20 minutes brushing and fluffing up the hair around the fetlocks (known as feathering by the old carters). Even the hooves had to be rasped and polished by the blacksmiths. The horse which had four white fetlocks had them polished up with thin oil to make them shine. The last task after grooming was to shine their coats with a large clean muslin cloth. What a sight for sore eyes it was to see them glistening in the sun, their coats like satin.

My dad always gave me a last ride on Delightful's back before he set about plaiting his mane and tail. He was so big and broad, his coat was so glossy that when he moved, I would almost slip off his back. (What a great horse he was,) he knew me like a bad penny. He had seen me from a tiny boy coming to see him straight from school each day I idolised him.

When the horses were finally yoked up in all their splendour with their bridles, collars and saddles gleaming from all the many hours of polishing on the leathers. Their chains and hames sparkling like silver and all the bells, bobbles and flowers in place, we were at last ready to proceed to be judged at one of many shows that were taking place at this time of the year. One was at the 'Mystery,' a piece of ground of several acres, so called because, apparently no one knew who had owned it. Some called it Wavertree Playground, not to be mixed up with Wavertree Park which was really the Botanical Gardens.

Photo E. Chambre Hardman F.R.P.S. Courtesy of the E. Chambre Hardman Trust.

A typical float in a show

It was always a great day out at Wavertree Show with its many side shows and attractions. Beer tents were full with carters and their wives and all horsey types, each giving their opinions of the different entries. There were many classes that the horses could be entered for, such as show jumping, tradesmen's turnouts, high stepping hackney. Welsh mountain ponies and the mounted police doing their bit such as tent pegging, musical rides and the charge, always great stuff to see but my eyes were concentrating on the wonderful draught horses from all over the country. Larry Marr, a well known man always had giants of horses.

Billy Hall was one of my father's good mates. He and dad lived

13

and breathed horses. They would often compete against each other, but we always knew one or the other would be taking a prize back to the corporation stables in Smithdown Lane. After the judging and prize giving there would be a grand parade, always headed by the winner of each class. It was a grand sight to see.

After the show, each carter would make his own way back to their stables. Dad however always made for our house in Telford Street. We knew all our neighbours would be waiting for our return. Everyone wanted to make a fuss of *Delightful* bringing him lumps of sugar etc., some with their little cameras to have their photograph taken holding the lead rein. He was treated like a film star posing with all who wished to stroke him. *Delightful* was so conscious of his role as a star, he would not make water all day in case he splashed his legs.

After the show was over we took him to my mother's sister's home to show him in his glory and for some unknown reason he would let the lot go outside her front door. He did this every year to everyone's amusement (except Auntie Annies). After that, he would be taken on the rounds of the pubs, where the locals would be waiting for him to arrive, especially the Satelite in Juno Street and the Woodside, both Higsons pubs. These managers would give the great horse a tray of their best beer, which he mopped up with gusto, just like my dad!

When all the fuss was over, we had to go back to the stables, unyoke him and take all the finery off. Then we would unplait his mane and tail, feed and water him, then bed him down on peat moss in the loose box. We didn't groom him but just let him munch away and relax until we came back on Sunday morning. Then when we arrived we would groom him because on Monday it was back to work just like the horses who didn't qualify for the show.

One of Pellings horses dressed overall

Chapter Three

New Arrivals

One day, there was a lot of excitement at the stables in Smithdown Lane. Word had gone around that the five horses belonging to the Lord Mayor, plus the coaches brake and Rolls Royce were all to be housed at Smithdown Lane. The L.H.C. must have decided that it was uneconomical to keep the small stable in town going, when there was plenty of space at Smithdown Lane.

I remember the months of work moving ponies and horses around to make room for these new arrivals. One of the large harness houses was converted to make the coachman's house. The first coachman to come to Smithdown Lane was Mr. Oldfield, his wife and son Brian, who was slightly younger than myself.

Mr. Oldfield cut a dashing figure in his tweeds and seemed like royalty to me compared to the carters with their caps on the side of their heads. The Lord Mayor's horses were different to the shires. They were especially selected carriage horses all bays whose names were *Sydney*, *Jimmy*, *Michael* and *Cork*. They were really something to look at, not a bit like the ones bought later after the war years. There was also a special garage built for the Rolls Royce, whose number plate read AKA 1. The car was sponged and cleaned every day, whether it had been used or not. The chauffeur was such a kindly man with the air of a gentleman. He kept very much to himself, not even mixing with the rest of the mayoral staff. Also housed in the building was a lovely State coach, all gold with crimson cushions inside which was very seldom used as it had been drawn by four in hand.

16

A typical scene at the New Quay area 1929

Photo E. Chambre Hardman F.R.P.S.

Mr. and Mrs. Oldfield's son, Brian, led a rather lonely life. When not at school he had to stay in the yard, that is why he looked forward to me coming after school. It was a very lonely place when all the horses were bedded down and the carters had gone home. The big stable yard gates were locked, shutting him off from the world outside, no wonder he waited for me. I tried to interest him in stable affairs, but he saw so much of this life, he only wanted to play at Cowboys and Indians in and out of the empty loose boxes. He was afraid of the lofts; he was rather a timid child. Playing cowboys didn't suit me one little bit, I wanted to ride the horses and help Tom Taylor (the day cook) to mix the various horse feeds, and do my own little tasks around the yard.

Each day Mr. Oldfield would exercise two of the Mayoral horses in the *brake*[20] or *pole wagon*[21] as it was called. He would take them through Sefton Park and Greenbank Park then back to the stables and then take another two horses. This was a ritual that happened every day, even in this day and age, 50 years later, I see the two horses that now do the job, going through Sefton Park and it is sad to compare the difference between them. They look so forlorn, not like the high spirited horses of my youth, even the coachman is only a poor copy of Mr. Oldfield who used to look so smart on and off duty.

I must mention the Lord Mayor's groom. He was a small, quiet man called Bill Smith. He had a club foot but it didn't stop him from doing a marvellous job grooming five horses and looking after all the harness and the ceremonial harness which was kept in glass cases. He also had to wash and sponge down the ceremonial coach and the green exercise brake. His standard of work was so high no-one would ever be able to fault him, he was so dedicated to his work.

Of course the arrival of the Mayoral horses made extra work for the two blacksmiths (old Lou and Dick Radcliffe) who were real characters. They scathingly referred to anyone connected with these Mayoral horses as Royalty, even the innocent horses received that tag. It is worth remembering that all central corporation horses and cemetery horses were shod at Smithdown Lane. I would often stand and watch the big horses being shod, even to be allowed to watch them was a privilege as Lou would come out with some choice language when a horse was being awkward. He would look at me with a sheepish grin and say 'you didn't hear that did you young Woody, if you did, don't tell your mam'. I think he must have known my mam from a young girl, he was always asking after her.

The two blacksmiths worked very hard indeed, from early morning to 5 pm, no overtime for them. You could set your watch by them, even at lunch time the banging and hammering would stop at exactly 12 noon, and the roar of the furnaces would cease. Everything would come to life again at exactly 1 o'clock. Everything ran like clockwork, they had their own special lock ups which were regarded as sacred. When they were not shoeing horses, they were repairing huge iron hoops for the heavy carts and keeping up the stocks of spare shoes for all horses in the central area, these hung up in sets of four on the walls.

Monday was a very busy day. All the provender for the rest of the week had to be cut and all the corn crushed. In those days, even the mounted horses in Greenhill Road were supplied from Smithdown Lane. A young man about 18 years old named George Clinton who befriended me, used to deliver all the foodstuff to the outside stables, even for the animals at the University. George drove a smashing dun coloured Welsh Cob by the name of *Homer*, number 152. We called him *Teddy*, he had a curious little rat tail, but what a well developed little pony he was. I often went with George to the various yards on delivery days (this was during school holidays of course) to Greenhill Road, Chestnut Grove, Green Lane and the Richmond Lodge, Smithdown Road. I have never seen anyone even today, with such a fine physique like George he could have put some body builders to shame, he was as strong as an ox.

One incident stands out in my mind when we were delivering to Chestnut Grove. The order was two gallons of treacle, which was in a milk churn without a lid, which was put alongside both of us so we could hold it without it spilling. It was such a lovely morning when George said to me 'here Harry, you have a drive of *Homer* for a little while'. I was so pleased at the time, I felt as though people were watching this small boy driving a lovely turnout, when all of a sudden, *Homer* noticed the bridge over Picton Road which he hated as the trains passed overhead. He shook his head and tried to take off with me. I didn't worry as I knew his fear, and soon had him under control. In the excitement, the end of the reins were dangling in the treacle. They were so sticky that when I handed them back to George, the look on his face was enough to turn me to stone. I had to hand them back before he arrived at Chestnut Grove as he was the pony lad not me.

George had a lot to do on his own around the yard when he wasn't delivering. He had to groom Mr. Lee's pony, *Kit Kat*, which was called *Jackie*. He was a lovely chestnut pony with four white socks and a white blaze. Beside his many other tasks around the yard, he was responsible for keeping Mr. Lee's personal trap in tip top condition, he was as good as four men anytime.

Some Saturday mornings were a special treat. Being off school, I could go to the stables early, just after breakfast. On certain Saturdays, Mr. Lee would say 'Harry, go and tell George to get my pony and trap ready for about l0 o'clock'. I would run around the stables like a scalded cat to find George and tell him what Mr. Lee had said. He was not too pleased at having to stop one of the many tasks he had to do before finishing off at noon, as this was his only early day off. In the end he would say 'give me a hand Harry lad or I'll never get finished'.

We groomed *Jackie* and hitched him up to the sparkling green trap, which had two rear seats and a small door which locked with a shiny brass handle. We would lead *Jackie* to Mr. Lee's front door where he would be waiting in his Sunday best and trilby which he always wore. Sometimes if I was lucky, he would say 'would you like to come with me today Harry?' I couldn't believe my luck, to be seated alongside the Head Horsekeeper of Liverpool. Before we set off, he would send George for his own special driving whip, which wasn't needed but just finished off the look of the turnout. From the word go, *Jackie* would be off like the bullet from a gun, he was always mad fresh. We would head down Smithdown Road to Richmond Lodge stables, where George

Queen Square 1951 showing the Stork Hotel in top right corner.

Roberts, the Horsekeeper, was waiting to show Mr. Lee around the stables to inspect the horses and discuss things in general about replacements etc, and sick horses and any queries about work.

I would be holding *Jackie* by the bridle feeling very important, until Mr. Lee returned to the trap, then we would be on our way again. This time we would head towards Woolton stables. then on to Green Lane stables, to have a word with Mr. Boswell who was a large figure of a man, and a real character. He was always smiling, he must have weighed 20 stone at least. It's a good job he didn't ever attempt to sit in the back of the trap, or poor *Jackie's* legs would have left the floor. Mr. Boswell had a son at Green Lane, they were so alike, they looked like twins. Freddy his name was, and he was a comedian like so many of the carters. In 1930 the Green Lane depot was very modern. The horses could get a drink at any time in the stalls, there was a lever on the basin and when the horse pressed it with his muzzle, the water would flow into the basin.

I enjoyed going to the Green Lane depot, as I could visit some of the horses my Dad had driven in previous years which had been transferred there, and it was like seeing old friends, I couldn't wait to tell my dad when I got home, just how they looked. From Green Lane, we would then proceed to Chestnut Grove in Wavertree. There were only four horses stabled there and Jack Cross looked after them. He drove one of these horses who pulled a container round to the nearby shops on the High Street. He really must have worked hard doing his own job and feeding and cleaning around the stables as well. They must have been a marvellous breed of men in those days, they didn't reap a great reward for all their hard work. God bless them.

The time would now be getting on and Mr. Lee would light up his pipe, cover our knees with a heavy plaid rug, and head back down to Smithdown Lane. On arrival Mr. Lee would go straight into lunch and young George Clinton would sponge *Jackie* down and make him feel fresh and comfortable so that he could enjoy his bran mash. By this time it was time for George to clock off for his half day. It was a blessing that people working with horses were happy, the long hours would not be tolerated today, without grumbles and strikes. No matter what extra work or emergency cropped up, every man saw that his horse was happy for the night, no matter how tired he was, they are to be saluted.

After George had gone home on his half day, I knew it wouldn't be long before my dad and the other carters would be coming back to the stables. I always knew after a few minutes, dad would say 'I've saved a sandwich in my dinner box for you'. He knew how much I looked forward to toasting it on the long fork, in front of the cookhouse fire. After being out from early morning I was always hungry. The carters would often give me a lid of tea, while I was waiting for dad to return. After I had finished this treat, I would help dad to link the *brights*[1] and *gears*[2] and wash the horses legs and dry them with white sawdust, then brush the sawdust out with a *dandy brush*.[22] The huge boiler was always full and bubbling, even some of the women in the nearby streets would ask for a bucket of hot water, as their homes only had a cold water running tap, no hot water and bathrooms in those days. We don't realise how lucky we are today with all the modern conveniences. When everywhere was tidy, my dad would clock off and we would head for home, but my dad always had his first pint of the day at "The Matlock" at the corner of Smithdown Lane. I was so well known by Clare the Manageress, she always sent a glass of lemonade out for me, but I didn't have to wait long for my dad, he soon lowered his pint and off we went side by side, up the road to home, like two old buddies.

My mother would have a lovely meal waiting for us when we arrived home. After the meal I was ready for a bath and bed, to dream of my lovely friends the horses.

Summertime around the stables was an exciting time for me. There were new horses arriving all of which had to be broken in, to be fitted with collars and gears, named and numbered, all to be shod for the first time, then sent off to different depots as replacements. There were always plenty of wild cats around, some of which were beautifully marked. They must have found the stables and lofts a haven for hunting the mice and stray pigeons which they would stalk and kill. I used to love to see the many kittens that they were always producing. We would leave milk and food scraps at different points, sometimes you didn't see them for days on end, but the food was always eaten. They were so wild you could not handle them, even the tiny kittens would arch their backs and spit at you if you got too close. It was a nice picture to see the kittens playing with each other amongst the straw in the sunshine, but if mother cat thought that you were too interested, she would pick them up in her mouth and hide them in a remote part of the stables.

Even in Winter with thick snow and ice on the roads, the horses had to go to work. This was the time that the blacksmith would have to put special screws in the horses shoes to grip the icy sets[23] in the road. It was not uncommon for a carter to knock at a door and ask for some fire ashes if there was a bad icy patch near the house. In those days when roads had been salted and the snow had been shovelled into heaps off the roads and sidewalks, these heaps would be carted by a horse drawn vehicle and dropped down a large manhole directly into the sewer. This practice is never seen today, but it certainly worked well, and the roads and pavements were soon cleared of ice and snow. Many a man would have to return after the first flurry of snow, carters and bin men and road sweepers would have to report back to their various stables and depots. Some of them would only have been home half an hour from a days hard work and they would return to the depots, it was almost an unwritten rule that if it started to snow heavily, you would automatically report to your depot. Some men and horses would work through the night clearing the snow so as the early morning tram cars could get through and take people to work.

The corner of Lord Street and Whitechapel 1908

25

Chapter Four

Summer Holidays

Around about the first week in August, my dad always had his one weeks holiday which was given for one years work. Although he had to turn in to work on Saturday morning for half a day. As a privilege because you were starting your holidays they would allow you to swop your district for the yardman's job, which meant tidying up the stables and yards which allowed the holiday man to be able to get away early, just before noon.

This was always an exciting time for we three younger boys. The week leading up to the holidays we would be taken with our mum to Graces, a pawnbrokers and clothiers at the corner of Wavertree Road and Chatsworth Street. Each year mother rigged us out in exactly the same outfits which consisted of grey blazer and short trousers, a grey cap immaterial of the size as long as it sat on your head, a coloured celense short-sleeved shirt, an elasticated snake buckled coloured belt, knee length socks and new garters. Then when she was satisfied with our outfits, she would march us across the main road to the Bata shoe shop for our American baseball boots which were all the rage. They were really just a pair of plimsoles in the shape of a boot and rubber discs on either side of the ankle and long laces which always snapped if you tugged too hard on them. Some were white with black rubber facings and the ones we got were sandy coloured with dark brown rubber facings, they were about 2/6 (12½p) a pair.

The next step was to be taken to Jack Bells barber's shop in Overbury Street, where mum would say 'Plenty off for these three Jack, we are on our holidays next week'. Jack would cut it so short we willingly wore our caps for a few days. In those days the barber would hand you a pencil or a packet of marbles for your custom. Then we would be cheeky enough to ask him to change for another packet if there was not a red and white one in the packet, these were known as Parrots eyes and worth six of any other kind.

The morning of the holiday would duly arrive and we would be scrubbed and dressed in our holiday clothes and not allowed to play outside or sit down in case we got soiled or creased before dad came home. We would wait patiently for dad to have a wash and shave, which didn't take long as mother had everything to hand, hot water, a new Mersey Blade in his razor, his clothes on the bed ready to wear and his shoes polished. All he had to do was get ready.

After mother had given my sisters instructions for the week ahead (the girls were a lot older than us boys and were working), we finally stepped out of the house with a huge case which was carried to the tram stop. The only trouble was we had to pass the Woodside Hotel at the corner of the street, that is, we passed it but dad said 'My holidays have started' and promptly went inside to sample half a pint, and having sampled it, decided to have a couple more, so after all the waving goodby to our sisters, one hour later we were still only a hundred yards away from the house. Nevertheless we had started off, then dad, fortified with a couple of pints, would join us and we would board the tram to the underground railway where we boarded the train for Leasowe on the Wirral, a journey of about twenty minutes.

Leasowe in the thirties was all farm land and you felt almost in the heart of the country and when we alighted from the train we went down the wooden steps from the platform and walked down a long lane to a huge field which was behind Leasowe Station. All around this huge field were very large marquees and bell tents. Each marquee had a name and number and was permanently on site all summer. These were owned by people who would then

27

hire them out, furnished, all season. First thing was to find your holiday tent which would be fastened down with cords and the cord pegged to the ground. When you had unpegged the flap or entrance, if it was fine weather, you rolled the flap back so the tent was completely open at one end.

As the previous holiday makers had left that morning, the owners would arrive to get everything clean and tidy by lunch time for the next batch of campers. They would put fresh bed linen in the chest of drawers, a big water jug and basin would be filled with fresh water also bread, milk and a dozen eggs would be on a large table. The hurricane lamps were topped up with paraffin and a primus stove for cooking would stand in a large tin when not in use.

The ground was completely covered with duck boards. There would be a double bed for my parents and three camp beds. The bedrooms were divided by a canvas wall to make two complete rooms. There was a large table and chairs, and a cupboard for pots and pans and for storing food, also in the bedroom would be an old wardrobe.

The first thing we did on arriving was to hang our clothes up and make the beds with the clean sheets from the old chest of drawers. Then mother would get one of the primus stoves going and would make us a nice cup of tea while she stowed away all the tinned food she had brought to help out with the meals.

After a quick meal and a wash, we boys would explore round and chum up with other boys and girls on the site while mum and dad went for a stroll
to a country pub leaving us boys to get the next days supply of water in large jugs. There were three large brass stand pipes for water, and each family collected enough each evening for washing and cooking the next morning.

We would awaken to the sound of dad pumping the primus stove to get it going, then he would say 'Come on, one of you three can go for the milk and bread from the farmhouse' which had just been delivered warm. Oh what a lovely smell of bread, you

St. John's Market 1909

couldn't get back quickly enough with them so that you could have some with your breakfast.

After breakfast, if it was a fine day, the tent would be tied up and pegged down as we would be off on one of the long walks that dad would take us on. Along narrow paths, through meadows, over stiles enjoying the real fresh air which we appreciated as the other fifty-one weeks of the year we breathed in smoke and grime from the trains which passed under our house as we lived over a railway tunnel.

I was always exploring and having mishaps, and one such day, full of the joys of summer and wearing my best baseball boots and white summer shirt, I was running and jumping about, thoroughly enjoying myself about one hundred yards in front of my family, when to my horror I jumped into a still green pond, up to my neck in mud and green slime. By the time my parents saw me I was standing there dripping stagnant water from head to toe, but there was no sympathy for me. 'Trust you' said mother 'that's your suit and shoes ruined and we haven't been here a day yet'. I must have ponged because I had to walk on ahead of them, with my brothers giggling behind me until we got to Moreton. I had to go as far as I could into the river to wash the mud and slime off, and as uncomfortable as I was, I had to endure it until we made our way back to the tent for teatime.

Some years my dad would hire a gypsy type caravan which stood permanently in Frankby, down a leafy lane, with a real fire inside and a window in the roof right above our bunk type beds. We loved this holiday best as when you awoke early, you could watch all the farm animals and birds from your bunk. Dad was happier too, as there was a nice little country pub where the farmers and farm workers went in the evenings for a pint or two. My dad and mum would go for a stroll after tea, and let us accompany them for an hour, then after they got to the pub, dad would settle us on the benches in the pub's courtyard and bring us lemonade and Smiths crips, oh how we loved that treat.

There were lots of lovely rambles through the lanes, past China Plate Farm (this got its name because a huge china plate was set in the wall near the roof), through meadows to Hoylake or West Kirby. We never even saw a bus or a car. These walks gave us boys great appetites, which mother would have to satisfy with large helpings of corned beef scouse, and freshly baked crusty bread and big cups of strong tea. Then when the tea dishes were washed up and the fresh water collected from the farm ready for morning, we would be ready to get into our bunks, exhausted but happy.

Although we were considered poor (dad didn't earn much money as a carter, for the Liverpool Corporation) he enjoyed his weekend pint. My parents always managed to give us a little holiday in either Leasowe or Frankby or Llangollen. We were very lucky as some of my school friends never had a week away from Liverpol. They thought they were lucky if their parents managed to take them to New Brighton for a day. Some never even had this day treat, but would get 2d from their mother, one penny for four rides on the tram, one penny for lemonade powder to make lemonade with the large bottle of water which you would fill from the various taps in the parks plus some jam butties and a few boiled sweets, you spent the day in Woolton or Calderstones, arriving home about 7.30 p.m. fagged out and starving. If some of your friends had a penny to spend on the way home and you passed a fish and chip shop, it was more than you could bear waiting for them to offer you a chip. So when I returned to school after the summer holidays, I always had plenty of stories about the country to tell them.

Chapter Five

The Beginnings of Change

One day a large black cloud darkened everyone's life. In September 1939 the start of the war. This meant all different kinds of drill and discipline had to be set in motion. New faces were appearing at the depots as the young carters who were eligible went off to war. Some had only been promoted a few months from pony lads to one horse men and had just started to get a man's wage. It made me sad to say goodbye to the young men who had befriended me, sadder to say some never came back.

At this time, during the first few months of the war, all the stable doors and windows had to be blacked out. Special training had to be given to men, so that they could cope with any new incident that might arise out of the bombing of the cities. My dad had to go on a special course on how to deal with fire bombs and any horses that might get injured. This meant he had to work a permanent night watch, 7pm right through to 7am, but if the air raid sirens went before 7pm, as it did on many occasions, he would report as soon as the sirens sounded, often straight from his bed.

Everyone seemed to rally around and take things in their stride. Civilians had been issued with gas masks and children in their thousands evacuated to the country. All kinds of services were set up such as the A.R.P. and the A.F.S. Everyone of age seemed to be doing extra duties, some became street wardens, some special constables attached to the police and others had to enlist in the

Home Guard. Air raid shelters seemed to be mushrooming everywhere, in the streets and parks and in your own backyard or garden, if you were lucky enough to have a garden. Schools in certain parts of the city were closed due to the evacuation of children and teachers. Some schools became headquarters for fire services and A.R.P. Wardens.

The children who were not evacuated to the country got very little schooling. Some had to attend ordinary houses in the district where a sitting room could be used to teach half a dozen or so children for a couple of hours. My brother and I and about a dozen other boys used to attend St Marys Church where we had lessons in the vestry for two hours a day, three days a week. It was only with having a good relationship with our teacher who we knew and respected, that we were able to learn anything at all.

As the war progressed and things started to hot up, I still used to go with my father each evening to the stables, even through the terrible May blitz of 1941 when Liverpool was bombed continuously from 6pm to 6am for nearly eight days. The horses were terrified of the noise of the planes and bombs and incendiary bombs that fell all around the stables lighting up the area like Blackpool lights. Sometimes a couple of horses would break loose in the yard but with gentle soothing words, we managed to calm them down again. We found one of the best things to do during a bad raid would be to walk through the various darkened stables, stopping at each stall and call the horse by his pet name. Just a few calm, kind words by a voice they recognised was all they needed to pacify them. Then we would walk around to the back stables where the loose boxes were, to speak to the horses through the vents. They always seemed to like to hear a human voice. We couldn't take the chance of opening the loose box doors in case they bolted in fright with all the noise of the raids.

During all this, regulations had to be kept and my father had to turn his time key every half hour through the night at the big clock that stood outside the cookhouse. He had to do this from 7pm to 7am. This idea was dreamt up by some official who was in his bed (or air raid shelter). This was done every night just to make sure the man on night work didn't relax to much. Of course this order came direct from the Municipal Buildings, Dale Street.

Lord Street, 1908

Come darkness, after I had been walking around with Dad, I would start feeling tired, so he would select a couple of new horse blankets and make a bed up for me on the large table in the cookhouse. Then he would continue on his rounds and just look in now and again to see if I was all right. I must have dropped off quickly with the big fire going and the thick blackout curtains shutting me away from the outside world. No matter how heavy the bombing, I always fell asleep once my dad had made me comfy. Sometimes I would hear voices outside, it was Mr Lee talking to my dad to see if all was well. He would say 'is young Harry asleep George?' but he would always look in, and between half closed eyes, I could see he would still be wearing his pyjamas under his overcoat, such was his dedication to his job and the well-being of the horses and premises. Mrs Lee must have been very brave in that big house in the stable yard. Being childless, I think she liked to see me around to run the odd errand for her. She treated me as if I were her own. They were a great couple.

Morning always seemed to come quickly. Dad would wake me up to a lid of hot tea. I would look across to the big fire to see our breakfast was already being cooked, bacon and eggs sizzling away on big cooking tins. I would get off the table, get washed by the big white sink in the corner over which stood a large mirror. The stable soap was so strong it nearly took the skin off you, dad had no need to ask if I had been washed, he could smell that I had! My hair was always sticking up like a cocks comb, then I would get dressed.

After we had finished breakfast, it would still only be about 6am, so we would give Spud a hand to feed all the horses. Then dad would clock off work, and home we would go, to see how much damage the bombing had done during the night. Early morning workers would be emerging from the shelters after a bad blitz. How some people managed to go straight to work and worry about being on time after a night in the air raid shelters, also do a full days work knowing that you might not get any sleep the next night, is a tribute to their courage and tenacity; heroes every one of them.

The pattern every day was the same for my dad and I. As we got nearer home, we would meet the people emerging from the shelters in St Annes Church school in Overbury Street. Often as not meeting our own family and we would go home together, mine being the only clean face amongst them. On arriving home, my dad would go for a lie down, while I made the fire for my mum, which meant raking out the previous nights ashes, which were put into a big square biscuit tin to be taken down to the bin. This saved you from having to make the trip with the shovel down to the bin several times. After raking, I would get the previous days papers and plenty of firewood, some nice sized pieces of coal, plus any old pieces of candle that had been left from the night before (remember, we couldn't have the lights on), then put a match to the lot. You then opened the oven door right back so that it was in front of the fire bars, put a large sheet of newspaper against it and it would help make a good draft to get your wood and coal alight. In ten minutes you had a lovely bright fire, just right for sitting in front of with a big cup of tea and a piece of dripping toast with plenty of salt on. This helped to soothe away the fears of the night before. While we were enjoying our butties, my mother was getting breakfast for my four sisters, who would soon be on their way to work. Three of them worked in Paton Calverts in Binns Road and one worked in a fruit shop in Lodge Lane. My two elder brothers were away at war so my younger brother and I had plenty of care and attention from my four sisters. If there weren't any lessons to attend that day, we would run errands for mum, but sometimes I think I was more of a hinderance to her. She was a fine big lady and we all loved her very much, even if we did get a good hiding now and again for misbehaving. She must have had her work cut out trying to look after a large family with all the rationing and shortages and us with good appetites but we never seemed to be without, and for all her efforts, I am, and will always be forever grateful.

After sleeping in the cookhouse for several months, I was quite surprised when dad said 'I will ask Mr Lee if you can use the office and sleep under one of the large desks'. I didn't think Mr Lee would give his permission, but he did and thought it was a good idea. I heard him say to dad that it would be more comfy for young Harry. Walking home with dad, he told me the reason he had asked for me to sleep in the office was that one evening he

Goree Piazzas, 1919

just looked to see if I was asleep and put the lights on for a moment and I was fast asleep but that he nearly took fright as I was covered in cockroaches. Even today I shudder at the thought, no wonder dad wanted me moved. It was much better in the office, there was always plenty to read and large ledgers to look at with all the facts and figures and secrets and many personal entries not to be seen by anyone, especially a schoolboy. They were fascinating to read, four of these ledgers became my pillow each night under the desk. If Charlie the clerk had thought for one minute that I was looking at his daily entries, he might not have been so friendly, but I did no harm, just a small boy being nosey.

It makes me sad when I walk around the city and the outlying districts to see the amount of rubbish strewn about, yet with all the modern machinery and lorries, the council don't seem able to cope. It was never like that when we had horse drawn vehicles. I can remember when the container was full, a Pagefield Lorry would arrive; always on time. It would lower the empty container down on two ramps with two wire ropes attached, it worked off the engine and was fascinating to watch. After the driver had lowered the empty container, he hauled up the full one, then the carter backed on to the empty container and set off again to continue his round, therefore, no time was lost. These days when the lorry is full, the gang have to wait until the lorry goes away to the tip to be emptied, I would say the system is not as efficient as years ago. Another thing that doesn't seem to happen these days is that we never see the gutters or drains of main roads cleared. This was a regular sight done by horse drawn vehicles. The night horses would pull a large brush wagon through the main roads in the city during the night. The carter would sit on an iron seat, then set the brush into motion so the city was swept clean before early commuters got into town. Even the city markets were kept clean. No skips were left lying around for days on end and stall holders got a good service.

In those days the markets were serviced by an old carter named Jimmy Taylor who was based at Gascoyne Street in Vauxhall Road. Jimmy's job was to service and keep clean the old St Johns Market. There used to be a space in Market Street where you could garage the empty horse wagon under the main floor of the old market, so all the traders had to do was to brush their stall and throw all the rubbish down a chute straight into Jimmy's wagon. When it was full, Jimmy just removed the loaded one out and replaced it with an empty one, then he carted the one with all the rubbish in to Chisanhall Street off Vauxhall Road where it would be (kecked) tipped into waiting barges to be taken away. (What good planning) Jimmy also serviced the town centre, keeping all the pubs, hotels and offices free from rubbish.

Even Sunday mornings had their characters. There used to be the old salt man from Gloucester Place in Low Hill. He would walk the streets with his pony and cart shouting 'Salt, salt, salt'. It was sold by the lump so he just cut what size lump you required with a saw. Then the old Jew man with a long beard and battered old Homberg hat would knock to see if any knives could be sharpened. He worked on an old contraption which he pushed from street to street working hard in all weathers. Then there was the sandstone man, who sold bottles of soft soap called *Aunt Sally*, plus *dollybags*[19] and bleach. He carried a large hammer on his pony and cart to break a piece of sandstone to your required size. He was such a funny old man always unshaven but never seen without his Derby hat which he treasured. Boistrous boys would try to knock it off, but never succeeded (I used to think that it was glued on).

Then there was the Indian silk toffee man who carried a large box which hung from his neck and contained strands of white toffee which looked like a silken string. He drew your attention to his presence in the street by ringing a large brass handbell and shouting 'Indian Toffee good for belly ask your mammy for a penny'. We children would surround him, asking for samples which he gave at first until he realized that he was giving away more than he was selling, talk about innocents abroad, he couldn't have made much of a living. He soon realized after a short time coming to Edge Hill, that it was all taken in good sport, I wonder what ever happened to that type of toffee so very fine and delicate and sweet. Oh what pleasures you could buy for a half penny in those days. For two jam jars we could get a ride on a roving roundabout swing.

Liverpool had many special characters during the war years even in Edge Hill where I spent my childhood, such as Mary Jane Perks, who always wore a mans cloth cap and only had one hand and a stump of a hand, but she could fight like a man if the argument in the beer house which she was often in, got out of humour. Her one hand seemed to give her extra strength and she would tackle anyone, no matter how big. She always wore a cap because women were not allowed into beer houses and they could only get served if the publican turned a blind eye. If a policeman entered, the publican could always say he didn't notice it was a woman. Another well known woman was Sally Schofield. She was built like a barn door and was twice as hard as she looked. She was married to a sailor and lived in Goulden Street. When war came she joined the A.T.S. When she and her sailor husband were on leave at the same time, it was like two armies doing battle outside Maggie Lees pub, the Craven Heifer. Sally would roll up her sleeves and display her tattoos, and heaven help any poor soul who tried to interfere with the fight. I cannot recall even once that her husband came off best or anyone else for that matter, she was so strong. I would have hated to have been under her supervision at camp!

There was also Tommy Munroe, a giant of a man. He used to take to the road, no-one knew where he lived, he was always very clean even in winter. He would walk for miles with his big copper jug hanging from his belt for making his tea when it was brewing up time. Sometimes you wouldn't see him for months on end, then, out of the blue on a nice summer day, he would arrive at Smithdown Lane stables for his lunch and a wash in the boiler house. He used to use the strong horse soap to wash with, no-one would check or question him as he had been known to run amok like a wild bull so the people at the stables just left him to do his own thing as he would soon be off again, striding away without a backward glance. He was one of the first people I ever saw using *Duraglit*⁶ wadding on his copper jug, in fact he condecended to offer me a piece to clean my dad's buckles and brasses. I never knew what became of him after the war, he just disappeared, never to return to the area again.

Then there was Rupert Gray, the lamplighter, who lived close to

40

Railway horse Chandos Street Stables

41

us in Helena Street. All the children knew him and would follow him around as he lit all the street gas lamps with his long pole with a hook on the end. He never seemed to get annoyed with the children following him. There were two or three lamps in every street, but we never followed him in early mornings when he came to turn them out as we were all still in bed. Those days are long ago but no-one was afraid to go out in the dark before the war, people were more content with their lot than they are today. Everyone seemed happy enough with what little they had. No-one had any of the luxuries that everyone has today, but your neighbours never seemed to be jealous. Everyone was helpful and ready to share what they had. There always seemed to be plenty of babies arriving in each household and there was no help in those days from the State. My mother and all like her, had to manage the best way they could, so it was good that there were plenty of good neighbours ready to help out in any way they could.

As each child grew, so their clothes which were still wearable, were passed down to the next youngest, shoes as well, even going to the barbers to get your hair cut, you had to take your turn as mother could only afford one at a time. 'Tell him to take plenty off' was the last thing you heard before going to Mr Jack Bells to have your 2p all off. In winter, if it was my turn to go to the barbers, it was always a crying match, as the shop always seemed so cold, especially if it had been snowing. Mr Bell tried to made it easy for you by warming those terrifying clippers which dragged the hair at the back of your neck. He kept the clippers on the hearth by the fire in an old Squirrel fruit gums box. If we were patient getting our hair cut, we were rewarded with a packet of marbles. A long thin box with about six in it, it was all worthwhile if there was a Parrot Eye marble in the box, as that was worth six ordinary ones; not like todays hairdressers where it costs the earth to get your hair attended to.

42

Central Station main entrance Ranelagh Street 1900

43

Chapter Six

The Start of Working Life

On leaving school at 14 years of age, to my disappointment there were no vacancies at Smithdown Road stables. My ambition had always been on driving the mail ponies and my heart sank, but I applied to Suttons the Carriers. They had a few van horses which were stabled near our home in Overton Street next to the Billiard Hall which was run by Cecil and Ted Robinson who lived in the house alongside the Hall. I left school on the Friday at 4pm and then dashed down to Suttons Head Office in Wood Street in the centre of Liverpool. I was terrified to go in and walked around the block about three times before I found the courage to go in and ask if they had any vacancies. Suttons employed a number of young boys as cart lads and van boys. They had about twelve horses and a small fleet of Bedford Vans and some Fordsons and they used to deliver all over town and the Wirral. I remember, on applying for the job, I had to see a Mr Jack Gresham, the depot foreman whose office was stuck away in the corner. The premises were very old and dark, but a hive of activity. I knocked on the door of Mr Gresham's office and a grumpy voice said 'Come in'. I nearly ran out again when I caught sight of the man about to interview me. He was smaller than I was with a big blue nose and spectacles. He had on a long grey dust coat which almost touched the floor. He looked at me straight in the eyes and in a loud voice that made me tremble said 'What do **you** want?' I said innocently that I wanted to drive one of the horses. He took one look at me and burst out laughing 'You, drive one of my horses, don't make me laugh. You have only just left school and you're asking me for a mans job'. By this time my knees had turned to jelly, he terrified me, but he continued 'If you want a job as a van boy, come to the depot on Monday morning at 8 o'clcock and don't be late. Also bring your dinner with you as I don't know yet where you will be at dinner time. Your wages will be 13/8d (68p) per week Monday to Saturday noon, if you work late on Saturday you get an extra shilling (5p)'.

I dashed out of the dark depot into the light again. My legs wouldn't carry me home fast enough to tell my mother I had got a job. She couldn't believe that I had gone straight from school to get the job. All weekend I was a dither thinking about having to face Mr Gresham on Monday morning.

Monday morning seemed to arrive earlier than usual. I was wide awake when my mother came to call me. I had always been an early riser because in the next street to ours there was a dairy which kept its own cows. Ernie Hudson the dairyman, was always up and around early delivering milk in 1 pint and ½ pint milk cans, which made an almighty noise in the early hours, plus the fact that he always wore clogs with irons on the soles and heels, tied with string for laces. He was a great yodeller and as strong as an ox into the bargain. In winter and summer alike, he only ever wore a pair of dungarees and short sleeved shirts. So what with Ernie and his yodelling and the clatter of his milk cans and clogs, and the thought of facing Mr Gresham, no wonder I was wide awake when mother came to call me.

I came downstairs to a blazing fire in the blackleaded grate. Mother always had a good fire blazing up the chimney before anyone stirred in the house, except my father who was always up and out before dawn. After having a bit of breakfast which consisted of a cup of tea and toast with dripping and salt, I headed out to work with my parcel of sandwiches under my arm. There were no buses in those days just the old reliable trams, which rattled to and from the city in all their glory. I came out far too early for work so I didn't bother with the tram but walked to the Wood Street depot. Naturally I was the first person there, I was so keen on starting I was making sure I wasn't late.

By the time Mr Gresham arrived to open up, there were quite a few van boys waiting as well. I stood on my own not knowing what was expected of me at first. After about 15 minutes, I was allocated to a tall man in a boiler suit who I soon found out was very deaf. He was to be my driver and show me what to do. The work was hard but enjoyable. We left the depot delivering parcels all over Liverpool and districts, each day a couple of large Leyland wagons would arrive from Manchester which had to be unloaded by hand. No stacker trucks or pallets, just the sheer energy of young boys. You thought you would never empty them, they were so long and full of hundreds of parcels.

There were also horse-drawn wagons which came from Edge Hill railway station, bringing all the parcels from Suttons Golden Lane depot in London to be sorted and delivered by our transport. All the parcels had to be put into districts before the carters started to load their own wagons. The longer it took to unload the later we got out on to our own round, and the later you finished. Sometimes it was 7 or 8 o'clock in the evening before you could start to make your way home. This was a normal day, not overtime which was unheard of. The rule was, finish your round and then go home, so in the end, the drivers would have the van boys running like greyhounds in and out of the shops. Luckily I had made friends with a horse driver named Larry O'Brien

The older boys would take the mickey out of the younger ones as they knew all the dodges and easy rounds. If they were put with a driver they didn't like or on a heavy round, they would arrive late in the morning, hoping one of the new boys had been told to take their place. Sometimes it worked, but Mr Gresham nearly always saw through their little schemes. They would play jokes on the younger boys by telling them to put parcels in the wrong districts causing confusion amongst the clerks. It didn't worry me too much as I didn't fall for their tricks, having been around working men and bosses since I was small.

The week passed quickly and I was very excited when Friday arrived, my first pay day. Everyone had to queue up outside the office, while Mr Drooker the Manager, entered your name and amount earned in a large ledger. When called, you entered the

46

office, closed the door behind you and when you signed your name, Mr Drooker would count the money into your hand, no wage packets. When I went in, he said 'Well son, here are your first week's wages' which he counted into my hand. My eyes nearly popped out of my head, he had paid me 14/8d (73p). I looked and said 'But Sir, I thought I was on 13/8d (68p) per week', he said, 'Yes you are,' but you have been on a very heavy district without complaining, keep it to yourself. Goodnight lad, see you in the morning', which was Saturday and included in our working week. I could not get home fast enough to tell my mam. 'Good lad' she said when I handed her all my wages, then she gave me half a crown (12½p) pocket money plus a wink and a smile. She told me to go and wash my hands and that she had got something special for my tea. When I took my place at the table, she put a large steaming suet pudding in front of me with lashings of syrup sliding down all over it. At that time it was one of my favourite dishes, but I soon found out they were hard to face two or three times a week. My mam thought she was spoiling me, no wonder I have never tasted one since those days, I must have had enough to last me a lifetime.

Chapter Seven

My First Horse 'Victor'

As time went on, the job became easier for me. I was developing into a strong lad. One day the Manager sent for me. I thought I must have displeased one of the foremen. I went in expecting a ticking off, but to my surprise, Mr Drooker said 'Sit down Harry. Mr Gresham and I have given special thought to you. We have noticed how much you like horses and the interest you have shown in them. Some of our older drivers say you have more experience with horses than they have.' So I told him about my father and his show horses and the stables where I spent my time after school and could ride and drive them. He said 'That's settled then, from Monday I am making you our youngest ever Horse Driver. It was company policy that you had to be 21 years old before you were allowed to drive a horse around the town. 'Report to Overton Street stables on Monday. There is a spare horse called *Victor,* he's a bit wild, nobody wants him, see what you can do with him and the best of luck. Oh, and by the way, your wages will be £2.3s (£2.15p) a week, a mans wage from now on.' I thanked Mr Drooker and Mr Gresham, whom I later became very fond of, he wasn't the ogre I had imagined he was.

Mr and Mrs Gresham lived in a nice house adjoining the stables in Overton Street. He looked after the horses as well as being one of the foremen down at the depot in Wood Street. His wife also worked in the stables, feeding the horses and brushing out the stable yard after the horses had left for the depot. She did this every day for less than 5/- (25p) per week. She was a kindly soul

48

and I used to feel sorry for her when I saw the blisters on her hands. In fact it upset me enough for me to go to the saddlers in Wavertree Road. I explained to Mr Davis the saddler, what I wanted and he made up some working gloves out of the soft scrap leather he had. Mrs Gresham was more than delighted and always wore them when brushing the yard thereafter.

The author attending to his horse

Monday morning couldn't come fast enough for me to see what kind of horse and harness I would be given. When I arrived I got some nasty looks and mutterings from the older men who had quite a bit of service in. It did not worry me one bit, as I knew how to groom and harness a horse and drive with confidence. No-one came to welcome me or assist, thinking to themselves let him get on with it. I asked which horse was called *Victor*, but just then Mrs

Gresham called me to give me a new *dandy brush*[22] and *curry comb*[24] and pointed out *Victor* to me. He was a nice looking bay Cob with a white blaze and three white legs. She told me he had been ill-used by many drivers so he had a nasty reputation. She said to be careful as he might try to bite and pin me against the *boston*[15]. *Victors* coat was in a terrible state with neglect, as having no driver no-one had bothered to clean him. I groomed him for about half an hour then it was time to go to the depot. I turned to ask one of the stone-faced drivers where the harness was for this horse. 'There isn't any' was the curt reply, 'you will have to make some up from the oddments in the loft'. I was getting quite despondent, thinking this is a fine start, everyone's only interested in themselves. I climbed up into the loft which was filthy and full of cobwebs and managed to put an old set together as quickly as I could. A good job I knew what I was looking for. What a sight it looked on that bright Monday morning, all the brasses were green mouldy, the leathers were white with grease. It had been in the loft for years. I was ashamed of the turnout when I arrived at the depot, nothing seemed to fit, even the wagon that was left for me was rattling and squeaking for the want of oil and grease in the wheel caps. We must have looked a sorry sight that first morning, but no-one else seemed to notice, if I had arrived with an old elephant I don't think they would have looked up. My first intention was to see the Manager and explain the state of everything, but he just smiled and said 'Do you best for a day or two and we will try and sort something out'.

I was then allocated a district and I went and loaded up, then went on the road delivering. I was given a van boy who was my own age so we got on well together. *Victor* was very keen as he had been in the stables so long. When we got to the centre of town I started to notice his bad habits, such as stopping dead and backing up at major crossings and the start to take off like the bullet from a gun. I could see that he had been badly broken in, no wonder no-one wanted him. Anyway I was patient with him and by the end of the day he looked like a white horse, he was lathered with sweat from head to tail with all the excitement and noise of the city streets.

I was glad that my first day had passed without any real mishap.

Water Spinkler, Great Charlotte Street, 1907.

When I got him to the stables, I washed him all over and dried and groomed him and then bedded him down for the night. I was glad to get home for a good wash and something to eat (dumplings again!) I had to smile to myself when they were placed in from of me yet again, but I didn't complain. After what I had been through that day, I was glad to get to bed, but sleep didn't come easily, my mind was searching for ways of trying to improve that horrible set of harness and gears. A nervous horse and a squeaky wagon, I knew I had quite a task ahead of me before my turnout could even remotely resemble my fathers.

The next few days I concentrated on getting the horse and harness up to standard, staying behind after my working day was over, grooming, grooming and still more grooming. At last I started to see the results of my labours. *Victor's* condition was improving and I wasn't so ashamed to drive him around town. I started to look around for spare harnesses to make up a decent set. I began to take the harness home at weekends and with my fathers help, we managed to turn a dirty, mouldy set into something that looked as if it was out of a glass case. Now I could start to hold my head up when I drove *Victor*, I even managed to get around the boss to sort me out a decent wagon. The one he sorted out for me, he found in Willeys the Wheelrights in Mason Street. It had a large iron seat set up high, just like the old covered wagon in the western films. It had one advantage, it had a footbrake, which was a great help to me when *Victor* started his old trick of backing up and then lunging forward. I then started, without him knowing, to take my father's spare *brasses*[25], *face pieces*[26], *loin straps*[27] and *martindales*[28], in fact anything that I could get out of his old chest without him noticing its disappearance, as he had so many, even rolls of braid and silk ribbon, which I used when plaiting *Victor's* mane and tail. After about six months, my turnout was the talk of the town. I had one of the nicest horses in the city without any help from the owners. Now the older drivers had to sit up and take notice, now that I had proved to them that I knew more than them about the care of horses. You can't buy the love of horses, it is something born in you.

People used to write letters of praise to the company saying how smart the turnout looked. Mr Drooker called me in his office to show me the letters and use to say 'Harry, you are a good advert for the firm, I wish we had more like you.' With more men being drafted into the forces he had to train younger ones to do the job. Two or three tried but if you don't love your horse or are not interested in his welfare, its not the same, so they didn't make the grade. That made them jealous of me because I was getting a higher wage than those who had been employed much longer. What they didn't realise was I was driving a horse and wagon which was quite a responsibility, while they were only van boys and I was still only 15 years old.

As time went by, the men realized I was doing a good job, so life became less hectic. In fact it seemed strange, as I now had a van boy who was three years older than me. He became quite interested in *Victor* and used to boast to the other lads that we had the best turnout. This in turn made other drivers start taking more of an interest with their horse and brasses, but they would lose interest if it rained for days on end as it made the brasses dull and green, but I used to polish them up every time we stopped while the van boy took parcels into the shop. Out would come my polisher, this had rubbed off from my father on to me, as he was a fanatic for keeping everying bright at all times.

Word had reached the main offices at London and Manchester about me and my turnout which was the envy of the company. *Victor* had come from Manchester with a bad reputation. He would snap at passers by which was not a happy situation for the firm, so we never left him unattended, in case of trouble. This was how I always managed to keep my brasses tip top, as the van boy would rather deliver the parcels than hold *Victor*, but with patience and kindness, and the changing of his bit, I soon had his tender mouth better again, as I had noticed one of his teeth was catching on the snaffle bit which had been sent from Manchester with his bridle, so I had it changed for a strong rubber one which I found amongst my dad's possessions in his old wooden horse chest. People could not believe the change in the horse.

One day, Mr Robinson the horse keeper at Manchester, came to inspect all the horses. He said that *Victor's* name had been *Harrogate* while he was with them and he was such a devil there they were more than pleased to see the back of him, so he was very impressed with the change in the horse's temperament and assured me he wasn't down at Liverpool to take the horse back. It seems he had come at Mr Drooker's request to see what a good job such a young lad had done.

I was always afraid when visiting horsekeepers came to Liverpool that one of them would go back with the idea of taking *Victor* away from me. The London and Manchester depots had the sway over the Liverpool depot because most of the big bosses were at London, but Mr Drooker who had been sent down from London to run our depot was my ally, so any correspondence about the horses went to Mr Drooker or Jack Gresham.

Part of my district for deliveries was around old St Johns Market, where they sold live poultry. Many a Saturday morning I would drive around after finishing my deliveries and buy a couple of pullets from old Joe who used to be the salesman for McCormacks Poultry. Joe was a character always slipping away for a pint of beer into the Duckhouse pub in Market Street. He looked the part in his blue and white striped apron, so I would look for him. When he had enjoyed a couple of pints, I was always sure then of getting two good laying birds which suited my mother down to the ground, as eggs were on ration (one per person) but it never affected us as we always had plenty of fresh eggs which mother sold to the locals who used to ask for them. These coppers she saved for me to replenish my stock. My birds were well looked after. I would pick up spare provender and straw from the stables, and market traders would give me bits of greens etc, so all the birds were happy, left loose all day to scratch and forage amongst the litter in the stables. I also had rabbits and pigeons and a pony which really belonged to my uncle, but he used to let me ride him around the streets. I was always buying some kind of pet, and mum was a great help as she loved animals as much as I did and would give me a few bob (5ps) to buy something I had my eye on if I didn't have enough saved up she never refused me.

Through the day, the narrow streets and back alleys in the centre of town became my world. I knew all the short cuts, like the back of my hand. It was a great help when delivering to the big city stores, whose goods entrances always seemed to be in the most awkward places, like back Bold Street, back Parker Street, Brookes Alley and Church Alley and many more narrow places around Dale Street, Whitechapel and Castle Street. If any of the other carriers were delivering in front of you, you could be delayed for quite a while so you had to have a card up your sleeve, hence finding out all the back cracks through the city to get there before them. One particular black spot was delivering to Browns of Clayton Square, whose goods entrance was in back Cases Street which led into Church Street. It was so narrow, the wheels of the wagon touched both sides of the pavement. You could always bank on the fact that by the time you got to the goods entrance, another carter would be coming in from the blind side of Church Street, the look of their faces when they realized I was there before them, they would have to back out and come around to Cases Street and come down the alley behind me. It was best to come in the way that I used to, as I soon found out that you could gain time which was all important when having to get through all my deliveries and collections.

Being called back home for lunch

55

Some days it was very miserable when it was pouring with rain, and you had to try and keep all the parcels dry besides ourselves. We must have looked a sorry sight, driving around the town in a covered wagon with myself on a hard iron seat. My van boy would get out of the rain by getting to the back of the wagon and standing under the tarpaulin. Even poor *Vic* looked miserable plodding through the driving rain, but still with his proud head held high. The reins would make my fingers red raw with the rain, plus the fact that *Vic* would also want to trot faster in hopes of getting out of the horrible weather.

The look on people's faces seemed to change with the weather. The old Hansom Cab driver outside central station looked fed up. He would sit in the cab himself if it got too bad. His horse also looked so miserable, his head almost on the floor. The poor thing looked like an ostrich. The photographer who was always outside the station would pack up and go home in disgust, with his tripod on his shoulder. No-one in their right minds wanted to be photographed on a day like that.

I felt so sorry for the pitiful flower girls sitting in Clayton Square in front of the old Prince of Wales cinema. The lovely flowers and blooms that they had been up at the crack of dawn to buy at the market would become a soggy mess in their cardboard boxes. The flower girls were not easily deterred and would stick it out in the pouring rain, their coloured headscarves stuck to their heads, but with their Macs and wellies on they never got too downhearted. Such a grand bunch of girls on good days when the sun was shining. They would give me the flowers that had broken stems and couldn't be sold and tell me to put them into *Vic's* bridle, but on bad days they would call out 'Its a rotten day for your job son', but it was worse for them, they had to make a living from it, I was at least getting my wages. Most of the shopkeepers were friendly and considerate. They would always offer you tea and cake and on bad days, would find an old Trilby or cap and an old shopsoiled Mac for you to wear. They were very thoughtful and treated you as a friend, especially Taffners the gents outfitters in Elliot Street and Neil's in Cases Street. I was grateful to them many times for dry clothes.

Arriving back at the stables on such days always meant extra work. I would have to dry *Victor* down with wisps of straw, making sure his ears were dry, then dry his legs with white sawdust. Then set to brightening the harness ready for the next morning. By the time I arrived home, my wet clothes would be drying on me. My mother was always glad to see me home on wet days, as she understood how I felt her having been married to a carter for such a long time. 'Get those damp clothes off and let me dry your hair' she would command, and taking a warm towel off the oven door by the fireplace, she would give my head a good rubbing until it tingled. Then she would tell my brothers who worked in offices 'Move back, let this lad see the fire and get the chill out of his bones, he's been in the rain all day'. My brothers must have been waiting for her to say this as it was a ritual on wet days. They used to laugh and say 'Let the only worker in we must all be statues' but it was happy banter.

Later on when I was warm and dry and full of my mother's good cooking, all the cares of the day would be forgotten as I looked forward to an evening out. There were plenty of dances to go to in the local church halls during the week, but Saturday was different and filled with anticipation, as we lads would dress in our "Roberts and Bromley" suits and loud Paisley ties, which were the height of fashion those days and didn't we think we were the bees knees when we went to the Grafton, Rialto or Locarno ballrooms where the big bands use to play. We looked forward to jiving to the Leslie Jiva Hutchinson Orchestra or Joe Loss, the Squadronniares and Skyrockets, Nat Gonella and Oscar Rabin all top dance bands of that era. At the Grafton Rooms, there was Mrs Wilf Hamer and her orchestra with Chips Chippendale the vocalist always in residence.

We would try to look our best in our new suits as we had to compete with the American servicemen who were stationed a few miles away at Burtonwood. The M.C. would not allow you to jive or jitterbug on the dance floor, but little groups of jivers would go to the corners of the dance floor and jitterbug to their hearts content. Most dance halls tried to ban this dancing, but it became so popular that they had to concede to demand.

Even on Sundays you could go to a dance at the church halls and local hops. Happy hours were spent at St Hughes in Lawrence Road and St Sebastians in Lockerby Road. For a few coppers, like 9d (4p), you could enjoy four or five hours dancing and comradeship. The best places like the Grafton Rooms were 2/6 (12½p), so you couldn't afford that pleasure very often. There was one that was called Plummies which was really the Edge Hill Ramblers Club. It was in a loft over George Dawson's stables. Many a local couple first met there. There was just a trio consisting of drums, piano and accordian but it got quite a bad name because of the fights over the girls. It wasn't the regular dancers but there were several pubs in the immediate vicinity and men would come in after pub closing time and cause trouble. It wasn't exactly made for tripping the light fantastic, the floor boards were full of knots and you had to be careful not to break your toes while dancing. I doubt if the poor horses below got much sleep with all the thumping above, they must have been very tired instead of rested by Monday morning.

If the police were called because of the fighting, they would just haul all the young men into the Black Maria, guilty or not, so we lads who didn't drink and didn't want our parents upset would pull the sacking back which was over the windows and jump down into the stable yard and land in the midden, not the nicest way to end an eveing but it seemed better to us than protesting to the police that we were innocent.

Another place we could spend an hour or two was at one of the many billiard or snooker halls which cost about 1/4 (7¼p) for an hour, so if four of you played on the one table, you could spend a happy hour for four pence each or, if you didn't have enough for a game, you were allowed to sit on benches around the walls and watch the others play. Soft drinks only were sold on the premises so no trouble ever started. In fact it was so quiet, you could just hear the ivory balls being played. One of the best local halls was in Overton Street and run by brothers Ted and Cecil Robinson. This hall had twenty-four full size first-class tables. Many a local man went for a couple of hours on a Sunday while his wife was preparing Sunday lunch. The brothers lived in a large house adjoining the Billiard Hall. The hall itself had an imposing doorway with long white marble steps and marble foyer with huge gates which reached the whole height of the entrance to stop any intruders after closing time. It was always kept very clean and the marble steps always looked lovely. Most of us boys became members, you paid six pence (2½p) and received a pink membership card.

Another good hall was in Tarleton Street in the centre of town. This was more for business men who would spend lunch hour and extra in the halls. This had several floors and the Manager would lead you to your table, like a waiter in a hotel, so that each floor would have different classes of players, beginners upstairs, the best players on the ground floor. Another well known place was the Marionette Club by the Old Hay Market.

By this time I was getting itchy feet at Suttons. I was not getting on too well with the new manager who had been promoted from Senior Desk Clerk. More and more lorries, especially the small type, were being acquired by the government for use in the army, so this was leaving more and more work for the horses to do and, as *Victor* and I had always pulled more than our weight, the willing horse always got the extra work. The new manager was used to lorries and didn't like horses and he liked me even less because I would stand up to him as he was putting too much work on *Victor* and that meant me as well. I was still only 16 years old, working a twelve hour day with no overtime pay, and doing more than the older men, so each day seemed to develop into an argument over the amount of work I was having to do.

Chapter Eight

The Docks Shire Horses

Things became so unbearable I just had to leave. It upset me greatly to leave *Victor* who was now a lovely horse and all the harness I had put so much effort into, it was the envy of the carters. I went home that night wondering what my mother would have to say about me leaving my job. I needn't have worried, she was very understanding and said 'You will get another job easily at any of the stables because, son, carters are born not made'.

As the days went by, I worried myself sick over *Victor* as he wasn't an easy horse to handle and that Mr Riley, the new boss, would do his best to find someone hard to break him, just to get even with me. Some men were like that and would take it out on the horse, but I needn't have worried because I heard along the grapevine, that *Victor* had become very distressed and lamed himself so he was not able to work for a few weeks. No-one wanted him permanently because they knew they would have to work hard to keep him looking as good as I had done. However, one day I did come across him delivering to Hughes Pawnshop in Brownlow Hill and I got the shock of my life to see this horse was a bag of bones. When the carter came back to the wagon, he was a man we knew as Fatty. I said 'What horse is that in the shafts?' and he went white and said 'Its your horse Harry'. I couldn't believe what I saw. I could tell by *Victor's* eyes he was finished and I said to Fatty 'I've a good mind to put you into the shafts and make your life as miserable as you have made his'. He eventually

Aquitania, Liverpool, c. 1920

told me, when I had calmed down, that he was the sixth driver to have him. He said Riley had given orders to work this horse till it dropped. My heart was heavy for weeks after; poor *Victor*, he had been the victim of my many rows with Jim Riley over the love of my horse.

I was out of work for a couple of weeks and my dad knew how restless I was getting, missing being in the fresh air and missing being with horses and the strong aroma which was all part of the scene. All around the stables, people offered me work driving light horses and traps around the town, but my eyes were turning to the Dock Road. This was a different challenge. I use to sit by Georges Dock gates and watch the big shire horses heaving and tugging at their huge loads along the Dock Road. I spent many a day watching the great teams of horses and steam wagons going to and from the various docks, with all kinds of cargo. There was no end to the many teams and horse drawn vehicles. Sometimes you could not see across the Road as the amount of traffic was colossal with the overhead railway going right along the Dock Road.

There were some great master carters all who had numerous horses and some very competitive carters firms such as Jarvis Robinson, Geo Davies, W.H. Harper, Garlick, Burrell and Edwards, the Liverpool Cartage Company and Union Road Haulage just to name a few, besides all the railway horses.

One day, as I walked home from one of my many walks around the docks I was walking up Water Street when the heavens opened. As I only had a short coat on, I was soon soaked to the skin and as I walked through the dimly lit streets, I knew that I must start working again. This time I wanted to work for one of the firms on the Dock Road. All this and many other things were going through my mind as I walked towards home. It was getting quite dark by the time I had reached Edge Hill church at the top of Wavertree Road. Not far now Harry, I thought, and you'll soon be home. What a treat it was to see a huge glowing fire in the grate. My mother's first words were 'You are going to catch your death of cold hanging around the Dock Road', but I was home, dry and warm with a large piece of hot toast with lovely dripping and salt sprinkled on it. I was happy and my mum knew.

Mornings never seemed to come quicky enough when I was young and energetic, nothing could keep me from the horses. Sometimes I would walk for miles alongside a horse-drawn wagon just to hear the rhythm of the horses hooves straining against their heavy loads, and the jingling of the chains as the chain-horses would give such an almighty heave, as much as to say to the shaft horse, come on, do your share as well.

It was always a comfort to a good team driver that he had a good shaft horse, because he was the mainstay of the team. He was the one who could hold the heavy load behind him under control, no brakes or lock chains being used down places like Newquay, just these giant horses sitting back in the *breeching*[16]as easy as a sailor swinging in his hammock.

When I walk around the same streets now I shudder at the experiences some of the old carters had to survive. Just looking at some of the streets off Old Hall Street and all the steep inclines around Bibby's Mill, and yet day and night, William Harpers horse were heaving and tugging, slipping and sliding on the old *sets*[23] in the cobbled roads.

The streets and warehouses around Bibby's Mill were a hive of activity. All the railway stations used to be alive with the various goods traffic coming to and from the docks. Sadly now it looks like a ghost town movie, with no Tate and Lyles, no Waterloo Dock Station, no Gt.Howard, Sandown Dock or Park Lane Station, nor any CLC Station, Brunswick Dock, no Great Western Railway depot at Mann Island, no Coast Lines Dock from West Canning, West Princes, East Princes, Trafalgar West Bramley Moor, Nelson and Victoria Docks, what a state poor old Liverpool seems in now, after being such a world famous port.

The number of Elder Dempster boats in the South Docks from Harrington to Kings discharging their loads had to be seen to be believed. Loading or discharging for the West coast of Africa, boats with names like the Tarkwa, the Tamele, Mary Kingsley, David Livingstone, Sherbro Sansu, Fulani, Diedo Accra/Appapa mail boats.

The Booth line sailed to South America from Kings Dock, the

Harrison Line sailed from East Brunswick and Birkenhead, the Palm Line sailing from North 2 Queens to West Africa, IOM cargo boats discharing at North Coburg, the Limerick steamers and Guinness boats from Dukes Dock. These were the sights and sounds I wanted to be involved with after I had left Suttons and *Victor*. I decided to try and get a job carting on the Dock Road which was known to carters as the bottom road and the overhead railway which ran above it, as the dockers umberella.

As this time my father was driving for the Liverpool Cartage Company who had stables in Grafton Street at the South end of the docks, and Cotton Street at the North end. Each day for a fortnight I called at all the main offices of the many team owners, like Jarvis Robinsons, William Harpers and David Rees in Lancelot Hey, but there were no vacancies for a pony lad, as most of the carters would try to get their own sons a job into their own firms, so I didn't stand much of a chance. So tucking my pride under my arm, I asked my father if he would ask a Mr Ike Bradley, the Managing Director, of the Liverpool Cartage Company whose office was on the second floor in India Buildings in Water Street. After about three frustrating weeks, my dad came home one evening and said one of the lads at Grafton Street had received his calling up papers and there was a job for me. I couldn't believe it, at last I would be amongst horses once more.

Monday morning dawned dark and rainy when my dad called me, to get up. It was just after 5am and seemed like the middle of the night. I must have looked a sleepy sight when I came downstairs but dad soon put me at ease with a large cup of tea. 'Now son, listen, don't worry about anything or anyone. When we get to Grafton Street, I will be around at first to keep an eye on you.' I managed a smile and said that I hoped so. Then we put our dinner boxes under our arms and set out to walk down Upper Parliament Street to get to the stables. It was too early in the morning to get the number 32 tramcar as dad always liked to be early for work. When we arrived at the stables, I was introduced to the Head Horsekeeper a Mr Sammy Robinson, who lived on the premises in a fine big house at the top of the slope.

The stables at Grafton Street were very nice. The loose boxes were painted bright green with large brass bolts and safety catches, also in the corner of the cobbled yard was a huge horse trough which filled up automatically when the water fell below a certain level. It was also lined so that when it was time to clean it out, which was done regularly, you just had to remove a huge plug and the water emptied out while you could brush all of the waste food away which some of the horses had deposited in the water while getting a drink. These stables were huge and modern, unlike a lot of the stables around the Dock Road, there was even a huge bath into which you led the horses down a ramp to wash them all over. Little Ernie Duffy the stableman kept the boiler going to provide hot water regularly.

I was rather nervous when Mr Robinson (Sammy) introduced me to Mr George Sumner who was the company runner. His job was to call around all the warehouses North and South of the docks, giving orders and instructions to the many carters and motormen. I was escorted up the slope with the two men, into one of the large stables, where most of the men and pony lads were about to bridle up, ready for the days work ahead of them. Sammy pointed to a huge shire horse in the corner stall and said 'You work old *England*, Harry. He has been working team-shafts for years and now he has become spare'. I didn't know at the time, but it seems all the pony lads took a great dislike to me right away, under the impression that I was jumping the queue and getting a man's horse and man's money. Mr Sumner explained that I was only getting lads money but was taking old *England* until I got used to the job. In those days a team would load six ton and over, a one horse five ton, and pony-wagons up to two and a half ton and float ponies one ton, 10 cwt depending on the type of cargo. That first morning at the Cartage Company was completely different to my job delivering parcels around the town.

My first job was to report to Steve, the work distributor at the C.W.S. African Oil Mill which was opposite East Queens on the Dock Road. There were quite a few teams and one horses waiting when I got there so I just joined the queue and followed on after them. My dad was in the queue with Luke and Gerry Moran, so I was in good company. After a while I was called to take and weigh the wagon on the huge machine in the yard. My first load was for

Cheshire Lines Railway at the bottom of Brunswick Street. I set my wagon under the chute at the C.W.S. and waited for the bags of cattle food to come down. I didn't have to wait long before the chute was full of 140 lb bags of pig meal. I started to panic, the bags were dropping all over the wagon. I didn't have a chance to get hold of them. My dad, loading further down the yard, had looked around to see if I was coping. Seeing I was in a bit of a panic, he quickly signaled to the loader upstairs to top sending the bags down. Everyone rallied around me laughing and pulling my leg about the mess I was in. I could hardly lift the 140 lb bags, let alone trying to keep the chute clear and load my wagon at the same time. After making a bulk head and straightening up the bags on the wagon, the loader came down from the loft and said 'Sorry lad, you should have let me know it was your first day at the mill. Let your dad show you how to load and you will be alright'. By four o'clock I had done three journeys to the various railways nearby. Every muscle in my body ached and my knuckles were red raw from handling the new hessian sacks. I was glad when Jack Moss, the runner, drove into Park Lane Station and said 'I think you have done enough for today Harry, take the horse to the stables and then go home'.

By the time my dad came home that night, my mum told him that as soon as I had eaten my tea I had fallen asleep in the big chair by the fire, and it was a shame to waken me, so he didn't wake me up until about 10.30pm after he had come back from having pint in the local pub at the corner of Juno Street and Harbord Street. 'How do you feel son?' he said, taking a good look at my swollen fingers. 'Its a hard life being a carter on the bottom road isn't it?' I looked at him with tears welling up in my eyes 'I don't think that I'm able to do the job dad, it's so different from what I have been doing. I don't mean the horse driving, I mean the flat wagons with no back on them to lean your heavy load against' (everything had to be placed in a certain position so that it would ride along the sloping cobbled Dock Road). 'Come on, get yourself to bed and let us see what tomorrow brings. it may be a different thing altogether tomorrow, you won't always be sent to the C.W.S.'

Dad woke me up just as early next morning 'Come on lad, lets see where we will be sent today'. I got up feeling a lot better after my sleep but my fingers were still red raw and my muscles felt like I had been on the torture rack. Dad looked at my hands 'They will be hardened by next week' he told me. I said shall I put an old pair of gloves on and thicken my hands with Vaseline. He started to laugh and putting his arm around my shoulders said 'You don't want the other lads to think you are a cissy do you? Just try to take it easy for a few days. They will be OK soon.

Chapter Nine

Learning the Ropes

Luckily the day turned out quite satisfactorily. When we got to the stables, my dad read out the work roster and said to me 'You'll be alright today, you are working for Elder Dempsters Sail Makers'. He told me I would be taking my horse and wagon to Crooked Lane off Strand Street and to report to Stan the head sail maker.

When I arrived at Crooked Lane and set my wagon under the hoist, a cheery faced man looked out of the loft and said 'Are you the new boy son?'. I meekly looked up said I was. 'Come up the stairs lad and have a lid of tea with me, and I'll explain what you have got to do today'. I climbed the narrow, dark stairs holding on to a thick rope which had been placed by the twisting banister to help you climb the many tight turns in the stairs to the sailmakers rooms above. The old sailmakers made me feel at ease while I joined them in their early morning tea. The loft smelled of tallow and tar. There was canvas everywhere in the process of being made into awnings and hatch covers, life boat covers and everything the large cargo boats and passenger liners needed. 'Now we are going to replace the hatch covers on the Sansu, she is lying at S.W. Toxteth'. All this sounded very strange to me so I told Stan, who knew my father and all the old cartage company carters, that it was only my second day. 'Don't worry lad, we will be coming with you to measure up the canvas. The ship only docked last night and we will load the wagon the way we want the new items to come off. Now lads, are we all ready? Let's get going'. Stan turned to an old hand at the game, 'Tommy, you help

Tea Shop in Clayton Square 1908

69

the lad to load up from here, then we will all go to the dock together'.

On arriving at Toxteth Dock, Stan said 'Now you are working for me all day, so don't worry yourself about anything. The gang and I will go aboard and strip the canvas off the Sansu before we can take the new stuff aboard, and remember, take no new orders from anyone, you are booked into the Sailmakers Department until I have finished with you'. It had started to rain heavily, so I was quite relieved to stay inside the shed with no-one to bother me. I seemed to have been standing-by for ages waiting for Stan to re-appear with some instructions on what to do. Finally at 12 o'clock, he appeared down the gangplank. 'It's dinner time Harry, make your horse secure and put his nosebag on. We have been invited to dinner in the galley'. I later found out from the other sailmakers that it was general practice if Elder Dempster staff were working by any of the boats at lunchtime, the galley cook nearly always provided you with a hot meal. I could not believe my luck, sitting in the galley having a roast dinner instead of my sandwiches, which were were in my dinner box, locked away in the Cart Box under the wagon, but they would not be wasted, my horse would have them at the end of the day.

All the sailmakers knew the crew, as sometime or other they had all sailed together, before getting a job ashore. I sat there fascinated by the tales they were spinning about different trips up the West African coast, names that fascinated me at the time, but in later years I felt I had been to them all. After lunch, we finally discharged the wagon and loaded up with all the canvas for repair. We all headed back to Crooked Lane and after unloading the damaged canvas into the loft, Stan said 'Well Harry, just put on your time sheet "Working alongside ship all day with sailmakers".' By this time it was 4.30 p.m. so I headed the horse back to Grafton Street a lot happier than I had been the day before.

When my dad came home that night, we had a talk about work and he said that jobs like that often turned up working alongside a boat. He explained that different departments booked you for the day, sometimes it might be the Engineers Department or the

Victualling Department but these were usually reserved for the older carters who had been there for years. It seemed so different working alongside the boat instead of carting the cargo to the various docks and warehouses.

As the weeks went by I was gradually learning the knack of loading and unloading along the lines of docks. Some jobs were quite pleasant, others were just the opposite, loading carbon black or wet hides was a dirty and smelly job, so was the job of loading stock fish and whale meal, but I got a good tuition from my dad and Dick Benson, the coloured carter who lived in Lydia Anne Street in Chinatown. Dick Benson became a legend all along the Dock Road. He had worked for most of the master carters before coming to the Liverpool Cartage Company. He had driven teams for old Luke Moran and William Harpers. If you were on a job with him he used to say 'Follow me if you can'. He knew all the tricks of the trade, even all the short cuts around the dock estate, so that he was always able to jump the longest queue for any boat. There were such places as the back of North Coburg near the old Fire Station where you could take a short cut through the Cockle Hole, given that name because it was a small opening just large enough for a one horse wagon to pass over a little cobbled bridge, where fishing boats would tie up out of the wind. By going this way, it would bring you out to the entrance of John Holts berth, the old tin shed which stood on its own. This brought you out alongside the entrance whilst the rest of the queue were still across at the other side of the bridge by the grain silo waiting to be admitted. Dick wouldn't go in to get his notes stamped right away, but would do a bit of acting, pretending to oil the wagon wheels or wipe his horse *Velvet*, named so because he was a black horse. Black horse and black man was his favourite saying.

When the Wharfinger would shout 'Next', Dick would casually walk up with his notes and Jimmy Lloyd who knew his little ruse for queue jumping would say 'Have you been there all night Dick?' with a wink and a nod.

As time went by, Dick Benson grew quite fond of me, and I quickly learned all his little tricks, he also showed me the correct and easiest way to load and unload my wagon. Without his

Liverpool Landing Stage, 1919.

kindness and patience, I doubt I would ever have learned how to handle difficult loads, such as fair ending timber and marrying up of timber which was loaded by hand. Large cases of matches from Sweden which were transhipped from North 2 Queens to the Elder Dempster boats which went to the West coast of Africa. Some cargoes were very, very awkward to load on a flat wagon and when loading, you always had to remember the camber of the road, otherwise it would all fall off. If that happened every carter on the Dock Road would know, as the word was passed on and what they called you wasn't very complimentary.

Joe Thornton was also very helpful and he and Dick kept an eye on me for my father's sake, as they had both worked with him for years. My dad always used to say that Joe Thornton was one of the best plaiters of horses manes and tails he had ever seen, but without the help and patience of these two men who taught me how to load and unload awkward cargo, I would never have survived my early years as a carter.

I vividly remember the time when loading five tons of sunflower seed out of a warehouse in New Bird Street, to be transported to the African Oil Mill for processing into cattle food. I had just put the lock chain around the wheels whilst I was at the top of Jordan Street, I then started down the hill. Half way down, the lock chain snapped away from the wooden support above the wheel. It struck me full of terror as I knew the old horse had no chance of holding the load back. The poor animal was right down on his haunches and there was nothing I could do to really help him. All I could do was to keep hold of his bridle. It was a terrifying situation as the load pushed the horse faster and faster down the hill, straight into the traffic on the Dock Road and into the path of the Mersey Docks and Harbour Boards shunting engines. I could visualise us both being killed but fate decreed otherwise and in answer to my silent prayer for help, and almost like a miracle, a motor driver spotted my plight. He jumped off his motor and ran up the hill towards us and started to pull the 140lb bags of seed off my wagon and jammed them in front of my wheels just in time to save us both. White from fright I managed to put the lock chain on the offside wheel. Thank the Lord that the man who worked for Charles Stevensons saw us.

After a few minutes, other horse carters heard of my mishap and came to help unload the wagon while I took the poor horse to the stables to be examined. Luckily he only had deep cuts on his hocks and after a few days rest, was as right as rain. I was sent home trembling and sick at the thought of what might have been. For years I still had a horrible feeling when I passed Jordan Street. Such were the working conditions in those days that no-one connected with the firm was interested enough to even enquire how I was, or ask me to explain how it happened, or to have other wagons checked for wear and tear on lock chains in case it happened to anyone else. As long as you reported for work the next day, no-one was interested. The Managing Director, Mr Bradley, at Tower Buildings was not interested in the horse transport section, his priority was to get more mechanised transport. The men were so in awe of Mr Bradley, if they were having their morning cup of tea, they would throw it away if they saw him coming towards them.

Chapter 10

Golden Dick

As time went by I soon got used to the hard, heavy work. One of the nicest parts of my work was to be ordered to go to the landing stage to meet the B & I and Belfast Irish Steam Packet boats. Sometimes it was the Ulster Monarch or Ulster Prince or the Munster or Leinster, which used to dock at the landing stage to disembark her passengers and cars and perishable goods. So on nice days it was quite pleasant work to have your horse and wagon on the landing stage, taking the cargo from the stage to either East or West Princes Dock. Many times I have towed a private car up the floating roadway with a docker sitting at the wheel of the car. All this was, of course, before the Mersey Docks and Harbour Board created a new cut through so the boats did not have to wait for the tide, but could come straight to their own berth and discharge passengers and cargo. In those days there were baggage porters in uniforms with a number on their cap, who pushed the trolleys filled with passengers' luggage from the landing stage to the taxi stand. Of course all these jobs vanished when the new dock was created.

However, when I was sent to the landing stage on wet days, it was a different story. Then the horses would get nervous with the clanging of the chains and the wind whipping the waves. The stage would creak and move and be very slippy and when the tide was out, the floating roadway would be like a steep hill so the horse could only pull light loads until the tide came back in and the floating roadway became flat again. Now and again, with belonging to the Cartage Department of Coast Lines, George Wilson from the Express Shed, West Princes Dock, would say 'Do me a favour Harry, I haven't a man to spare, will you put the nosebag on the old horse and leave him in the corner with the wheels secured and take these four greyhounds to Lime Street Station'. This was just one of the various jobs that made your day complete.

One special day which I shall always recall with pleasure, was one evening. I had just lightened a load at Huskisson Dock Station and had ten minutes to spare which I spent polishing the gears on the old horse *England*, but the horse was getting on in years and I couldn't do much to improve his looks. Most lads of my age on the Dock Road had nice flash ponies, so to be honest, I kept my head down when *England* and I passed them. On this evening, I put the reins on and made my way South to Grafton Street where I was stabled. On my way in I noticed a commotion around number two loose box. As I took *England* up the slope to his stall, Mr Harper called after me 'Make *England* secure then come and see me'. I knew I hadn't done anything wrong. To my surprise when I got back, the yard was deserted and the loose box closed. Mr Harper called me into the office and put his arm around my shoulder, saying 'Harry, old *England* has been sold, along with the other old team horse, but come and see what you think of this', and with that he took me across to number two loose box. 'Open the door lad, and have a look. What do you think of that?'

When the door opened I couldn't believe my eyes. There stood the most beautiful grey Welsh cob, perfect in every way. His mane and tail were plaited with wide blue and yellow ribbons and adorned with little pennants of the same colours. His fetlocks were all white and grey curls, which I had never seen the likes of before. As the door opened, he started to rear and buck, he was so full of life. Sammy Harper with his arm still on my shoulder said 'All the lads want to know who is getting him and I've decided to give him to you as you try to bring out the best in the old horses, so I know this one will be special to you'. He knew that I was speechless and full of joy, so he just said 'Go and tell your dad about him when you get home, and by the way Harry' he called as I was leaving to go home 'we've called him Golden Dick'.

Sammy told me this Welsh cob was rather special, he usually bought all the new horses, but Sir Alfred Reid the head of Coast Lines, had been passing through Denbigh on the day of the horse sales, and this grey pony really took his eye, so he decided to buy it for the Cartage Department of Coast Lines, which was the Liverpool Cartage Company in Grafton Street. As this had never happened before, he was to be treated as something special.

Delivery cart circa 1940

The next couple of weeks was spent getting him properly shod and fitted out with a new set of gears by Cloynes of Lodge Lane. They acquired a special wagon and the wheelright painted and lined it orange, black and white, the company colours, but of course, *Golden Dick*, who had never been away from the Welsh hills before, had to be introduced to his gears and wagon which at first he resented, not knowing what was happening to him. He had to gradually get used to all the sounds of the Dock Road. The noise of the M.D.H.B. steam trains shunting goods to and from the docks into the different railway sidings, also the clatter of the overhead trains, plus all the sounds coming from the river, all of which helped to make him very nervous at first; it took two of us at his head just walking him in the shafts through the dock estate and over bridges, to show him he had nothing to fear.

All through this training period he was upset and would not eat his food, which in turn upset me, and I was always looking for titbits to tickle his palate. If I was passing the I.O.M. boat at East Queens Dock, I would look out for a couple of fresh swedes from bags that had burst which I would chop up small and mix with his provender at lunch time. Other times I would take the nosebag into the C.W.S. African Oil Mill and go into the compound and get a scoop or two of cattle or horse nuts. These I kept to mix with his evening meal at the stables, just to try and make him eat a bit more. In the end he wouldn't look at the ordinary meal provided by the firm unless I managed to get these tasty extras, so I had started something that I couldn't stop. Quite a number of mills on the Dock Road, such as Crossfields Mill or Bibby's Mill and Silcocks in Great Howard Street, would have troughs where bulk mollasses and treacle were discharged into from the tankers, into the extract mill. All carters carried a bucket under the wagon on a hook, for the horse to have a drink out of during his working hours. On cold days, if I hadn't got any carrots or swedes for his meal, I would get about one third of my bucket full of treacle, then when we got to the stables, I would heat and pour this treacle mixture over his provender, which he would really enjoy.

After a couple of weeks, the runner for the company decided it was about time that the pony should get the longer journeys because he was so keen. So it came as no surprise that anything that had to be moved from the South end docks to Canada or Gladstone Docks up the North end was given to me. After I had lightened my load, I would then have to report to old George Sumner, who would pass the time of day with me for a while, then tell me to report to one of the Coast Lines berths, usually West Trafalgar, where the cargo had been unloaded and was waiting to be carted to various railway stations and warehouses. Sometimes it was cartons of canned goods for Reckits of Henry

Street, which suited me nicely, coming back to the South end. Henry Street was a bad street to get to, but *Golden Dick* had the speed to get up there. After lightening my load there, I would drop down to the Dock Road again to the C.W.S. Mill and Steve the Foreman would perhaps give me a handy load to take to Cheshire Lines, which would suit me nicely and complete my day on the time sheet.

Each day was a challenge, sometimes you were sent to a dock sheds which were very, very slippery, some were almost impossible to get into to unload. Sometimes it was chaos at the sheds, trying to get your load, especially if a ship was loading at the same berth. You would have to leave your sett to let the crane get the load for the ship, then try to get back with your horse and wagon to the sett you were in to resume loading. Some days were very frustrating, but other carters were in the same position so you accepted it. Some days, if you were loading outside, the trains on the dock estate were shunting in and out to be loaded and unloaded, so you would have to get out of the way until the train had shunted the loads in and taken the empty wagons out, before you could get back to your place again and finish your job.

As *Golden Dick* got used to the work, he started to put on a bit of weight (or beef as a carter would say) which made me a lot happier. On summer days I could really get to work on grooming him, keeping a dappled grey clean is a task in itself, but trying to keep it to a high standard meant a great deal of grooming and polishing. If it was a really nice day on Saturday, I would wash him all over, then finish him off with water into which I had put a Reckits Blue Bag which seemed to show the dapples in his coat better. I would leave the washing of his legs to the last, then I would dry them in white sawdust which I would brush out with the *dandy brush*[22] when dry. Then his fetlocks would be all white and curly and, in my eyes, he looked a picture.

Some days in the wintertime were really miserable because not only did you have the worry of trying to keep your loaded wagon dry, but you would also have to try to keep your pony dry and keep your brasses from getting too tarnished, all this while the rain was running into your eyes and soaking your shoes, but your concern for the horse was more important than your own misery.

North John Street 1908

Just as I thought the pony had settled into his work, I was ordered out one Monday morning, which was a cold, windy day. I had to go to the French West Africa Company which was situated in the Royal Liver Building. I was to collect thirty small cases of important and expensive export goods. On arriving at the Liver Buildings, the floating roadway side, I made the wagon secure by putting one lock chain on, then went into the building to report to Mr Lamb, the Goods Export Officer. After we had taken the thirty cases to the lift, "Old Andy" the goods lift operator gave me a hand to load them into the lift. When we arrived at ground level, we started to unload the lift and put the cases on a trolley to take out to the wagon. To my absolute horror the horse or wagon were nowhere to be seen. Panic stricken for the pony's sake I ran around trying to imagine which way he would go in all the traffic. I ran as fast as my legs would carry me to the floating roadway. The policeman on the landing stage, who knew me because I often had to unload the Irish boats, assured me that *Dick* hadn't gone that way. I then ran to West Princes Dock, and was assured by the runner, George Trotter, that he hadn't seen the pony anywhere around there. So feeling very upset I knew I would have to go to our office at North East Canning Dock to report what had happened. However before I had a chance to report, I spotted him standing there calm as you like outside the office where we used to get our daily orders. Charlie Stevens the clerk, took hold of me, 'Come in Harry and have a cup of tea, you look dreadful'. They were all amazed that the pony had dodged all the traffic with one wheel still locked. He had come up under the overhead railway, across the main junction of Water Street and James Street, had turned right at Red Cross Street to get himself on to the stand outside the office. We could only assume it might have been a liner blowing its siren or some noise he hadn't heard before had so startled him that he took off. I was only too glad he was safe and sound and we went on to finish our work by taking the thirty cases to the Mary Kingsley, one of Elder Dempster's line boats which was loading at South West Brunswick Docks. Needless to say, I didn't want many days like that.

Golden Dick and I struck up a very close relationship. The horse got to know every nook and cranny of the Dock Road. We would have lunch together, I never left him at lunch hour, I would give him a nosebag while I sat close by having the sandwiches my mother had cut up for me. Then, if I had fifteen minutes to spare, I would give him a wipe down and rub his brasses up again and off we would go to do our afternoon's work, feeling refreshed. If I left him for a minute or two, I could see his ears cock as he knew my footsteps. He always seemed to be looking for me. He was only happy when I was by his head. After a night in the stables as soon as he heard my voice saying good morning to other carters, he would start to whinny.

After I had been working with *Golden Dick* for about two years, I arrived home one evening and my mother said 'Harry there is a letter for you with O.H.M.S. on the front of it'. She knew what it was of course, because I had older brothers in the army. When I opened it up it was to tell me to report to Durranhill camp at Carlisle. You can imagine the sadness on my last Saturday at work before joining up. Having to say goodbye to Dick Benson, Joe Thornton, Luke and Gerry Moran, Harry Thomas, George Sumner the runner, old Ernie Duffy the loft man and Sammy Harper the horse keeper. All the men who had tutored me and helped me to be a Dock Road carter. My last goodbye was left for *Dick*, who of course had no idea what was happening, but my heart was aching as I left the stables. Just as I was leaving the yard, I was called back to answer the telephone, and to my amazement, Mr Bradley the Managing Director of the Liverpool Cartage Company was calling to wish me luck and to say my job would be waiting for me when I returned from the army.

Joe Thornton had the last word as I was about to leave. He got hold of my hand 'Here you are young Woody, take this, we've had a little whipround for you', and he gave me a little brown envelope.

As I left the stables, so downhearted that I couldn't lift my head up, I heard a whistle behind me and a voice said 'Aye aye our kid, how about taking me for a pint' and with that, my dad's arm came around my shoulder and he whispered 'The other carters have chased me to have a pint with you and they will clean and bed my horse down for the weekend'.

As I went to have that pint of beer with my dad, I knew one part of my life was over and I now had to look forward to a completely new way of life in the forces, but one thing would never change, no matter what happened, my memories of *Golden Dick* would always remain very special.

Dressed for a show

Chapter Eleven

National Service

It was a miserable Friday morning in November the day I had to go to Exchange Station to catch the train which would take me to Carlisle. I wasn't too happy at the prospect as I had never been away from home before, and although some of my friends had gone into the forces, most of my mates would still be at home, able to go to the local hops and dance halls, such as the Grafton Rooms, where we had spent many happy hours. I was also leaving my special collection of hens which I had taken an interest in since I was a small boy. My mother didn't mind the task of feeding and taking care of them as she always had plenty of fresh eggs from them and the odd meal for special occasions when one stopped laying. So I was feeling rather pensive but trying not to show it as two of my sisters, Lizzie and Mary both came with me to the station. At Exchange there was a high class buffet bar and when I had worked for Suttons, I used to deliver around Pall Mall and deliver to the little shops and kiosks on the station, so I told my sisters to wait a moment while I went in to tell the Manageress that I was going into the army, as she always gave me a cup of tea when I used to deliver. 'What are you doing here Harry? Are you back at Suttons?' 'No Miss Elliot' I replied, 'I am getting the train to Carlisle to join the forces and I've just popped in to say goodbye.' She was a very elegant lady and said 'Good luck Harry' and then she took two meat pies from under a big glass dish and put them into a white paper bag 'Take these, just in case you can't get anything to eat on the train journey'.

When I got to the platform it was chaotic. Army personnel were running around shouting out names and asking us who we were and where were we bound for. Then they took you out to the part of the train where you had to stay put for the rest of the journey.

Once the steam engine was attached to the carriages we knew we would be leaving at any minute and there was lots of pushing and shoving to get to the window and undo the leather strap that kept the window closed. Once the window was down and the whistle blew I leaned out of the window to kiss my sisters goodbye, trying not to look upset for their sakes. As they gave me a last kiss, each one pressed half a crown (2/6) (l21½ p) into my hand with instructions to 'buy some stamps and don't forget to write'. With that I moved aside to let another boy get to the window to say goodbye to his family. Then the train slowly chugged out of the station leaving a coach full of young men to settle down for the journey and get to know one another.

On our arrival at Carlisle Station it was like entering another world. The noise of army personnel and big trucks, people being marched one way then another was enough to intimidate the faint-hearted. Then a booming voice shouted 'All for Durranhill Camp step this way'. Myself and a young man named Ray Woodward who was immediately christened Ginger Woodward because of his red hair, both stepped forward together and this is the way we would be right through our service days.

We were packed into the army trucks like sardines in a can. By the time we arrived at Durranhill it was almost dark. We had to go through rigorous documentation and were given our service numbers, my numbers ending 968 and Ginger was 969. Then we were shown to our wooden billets, shown where we could sleep and then we were marched to the cookhouse for our first meal in the army, which was a pint mug of tea and a piece of boiled fish of which, needless to say, none of us felt like eating, I had a meat pie left so I ate that instead.

We only just seemed to fall asleep as the huts were so cold, when a voice shouted to us to get up as Reveille had blown and we knew in no uncertain manner that our "Army Days" had started.

The second day dawned and we had to wake up to the grim reality of army life. To start with we had to find our way to the wash rooms where you had to wash and shave in cold water. Even if you had not started to shave yet, you had to go through the motion of shaving. You were allowed 30 mins to get washed and dressed and make your bed and be outside your hut ready to be marched for your breakfast by 6.30 a.m. As we were still in civilian clothes we were told that after breakfast we would be kitted out with our uniforms. To us young lads who were very hungry, breakfast was a big disappointment. We got half a fried egg, which had been on a hot plate all night, one round of bread and one spoonful of beans, plus a pint mug of tea. At least the tea was hot and strong.

As about a thousand new recruits had arrived overnight, the place was a hive of industry. Some were detailed to see the Medical Officer, some to the dentist, others to the barbers and others to be kitted out.

When it came to being kitted out, we fondly imagined we would be measured for our uniforms. Instead, as you arrived at GQMS stores expecting a nice uniform, you were handed a large crumpled bundle, with the words 'That will fit you'. When we got back to the hut and tried them on, there were more creases in them that in a pound of tripe. Then a very smart N.C.O. was paraded in front of us and we were told 'This is what your uniforms must look like for Muster Parade tomorrow'. To say the look of consternation was on all our faces is putting it mildly.

When we managed to sort out our uniforms, our hearts sank even lower. We didn't know where to start, but when we put them on we all dissolved into laughter as we looked like clowns. My cap G.S. alone seemed as large as a three foot pancake and one of my pairs of boots I couldn't even get my feet into as at the time we were told 'No complaints, exchanges are impossible'. I had these boots unworn right through my army days.

But salvation was at hand for all of us recruits as into the hut stepped a very wide awake Corporal who had seen it all before. 'Never mind lads,' he said 'the last lot looked worse than you, but

85

luckily I've come to your rescue.' Our spirits rose at these kindly words, until he said 'I've got an electric iron that you can take turns in borrowing for a shilling an hour.' As most of us only had about half a crown to see us until pay day these words were quite a blow, but still all the shillings came out in the hurry to borrow the iron. As we couldn't all use the iron at once and no-one was going to trust anyone else to press his uniform, we put our names into one of the caps and you had your turn of the iron when your name came out. As the only plug was in the light socket and we had to use a blanket on the floor, to try and press the heavy khaki serge into the design of the pleats which all had to be regimental, I was quite relieved when my name was drawn out of the hat second only to Ginger Woodwards.

Never having used an electric iron before, as we still had flat irons at home which gradually got cooler as you used them, I didn't realise that the iron was getting hotter and hotter (no regulo on electric irons in those days). I was trying so hard to press my pleats in that when I lifted the iron up, a huge imprint of the iron was on the back of my jacket. To say I broke out into a sweat is to put it mildly as it was my best B.D. All work of polishing boots and blancoing webbing while they waited for their turn of the iron came to a stop, as they all gathered around to witness my dilemma. All sorts of comments were made, 'My God, you will be on a charge for defacing the King's uniform' was the first frightening thing I heard. I looked at Ginger, who was just putting his nicely pressed jacket on a hanger, and said 'This is another fine mess you've got me into' trying my best to make myself laugh, as I used to love the Laurel and Hardy films.

The next to use the iron learnt from my mistake and one lad sat by the light switch and switched it off when the iron started to get too hot, thus making sure that the same thing did not happen again. But as it happened, fate stepped in to save me. The stove which was used for heating the hut used coke, which had to be drawn daily from the fuel compound, and someone from each hut had to collect the daily ration. As everyone else was busy, and I was full of misery wondering what to do about my uniform, I decided to go for the coke ration to take my mind off myself. When I got to the fuel compound there was a private soldier who was being demobbed the next day and had been given this job for the last few weeks of his service. His job was to take your name and billet number so you could only draw your ration of coke each day. He said 'Are you one of the new recruits?' and I told him I was. 'Don't look so unhappy son, it's not as bad as it seems at the moment' but as I blurted out my tale to him, he started to laugh. 'It's your lucky day son, tell me your name and the number of your billet and I'll bring one of my uniforms to you tonight and hand in your damaged one amongst all my other kit when I hand it all in tomorrow.' I couldn't believe my luck and I almost skipped back to the hut with the coke, but about an hour later, doubt set in and I started to wonder if the soldier had been kidding me, but at about 9.30 p.m. when nearly everyone had gone to the N.A.A.F.I., sure enough he came to the door with his pressed uniform. When I showed him my ruined one he said 'Don't worry, when I've finished folding this no-one will see it tomorrow.' I was so relieved I asked him if I could treat him to a pint at the N.A.A.F.I. with the money my sisters had given me, so he came for a drink with Ginger and myself. I couldn't thank him enough and he never told me his name. He was starting a new life in civvy street the next day, but I never forgot his kindness. Needless to say, Ginger and I were the only ones to know what happened and no-one else ever shared this secret. Next day at Muster Parade, when we were inspected and checked, the rest of the squad were waiting to see what punishment I was in for, but like everyone else I got through the inspection with flying colours, much to their amazement and so it all turned out well in the end.

The next six to eight weeks at Durranhill were vigorous primary training, which knocked us all into shape. Every day consisted of P.T. in the gym then drill parades on the square and weapon training, route marches, country runs and guard duties plus fatigues for those who were put on charges, all this made us into fit youths. After eight weeks we were transferred to Hadrians Camp in Carlisle for advanced battalion training.

Hadrians Camp was huge. It consisted of a holding battalion and a training battalion. After ten weeks of intensive training we were allocated to our new regiment. Ginger and I and a couple of other pals were sent to the Border Regiment or the 34th Afoot as it was later drummed into us. Other mates went to the East Lancs Regiment or the Kings Own or the Loyals. Then we really felt part of the armed forces. When the N.C.O.s thought we looked smart enough, we were allowed a daytime pass to spend a few hours in Carlisle.

When Christmas arrived that year we were up in the Fell country at Glenridding This camp was nicely situated and must have been lovely in the summer, but in the depths of winter, in corrugated huts, we were perished all the while, even the stove in the centre of the hut didn't seem to give out much heat. We were glad of our Great Coats to put on our beds at night. At Glenridding we did night training and map reading and fell climbing, and using assault crafts on Lake Ullswater. The boys who found this course too tough were sent back to other camps as not being fit enough for the infantry. We were then sent back to Hadrians to join the holding company, there to await our draft to be sent abroad. We were all given embarkation leave and we arrived back home for the first time since the day I joined up.

After a pleasant few days leave with my parents, I had to report back to Hadrians, then we were told that we were being drafted to the Middle East and would be sailing from Liverpool. We were all issued with K.D. shorts and shirts and the next few days were spent painting our draft number on kit bags etc.

The day we set off Reveille was very early as we had to march from Hadrians Camp to Carlisle Station. The draft consisted of re-enforcements of the Loyals, East Lancs, the Kings Own and the Border Regiment. By the time we pulled into the Riverside Station, other regiments from different parts of Britain were all converging on Liverpool to embark on the troop ship, the S.S. Devonshire, which was berthed at Princes landing stage.

It was very frustrating for all the Liverpool lads to be so near yet so far from home, as none of us had been able to tell our families that we were going abroad, but once again, as luck would have it, as the train pulled into Riverside, which reminded me so much of my days working at the Cartage Co., when out of the blue someone was calling my name and there was George Stone, a motor driver for the Liverpool Cartage Co., who was delivering to the Belfast boat at West Princes Dock. As he was so surprised to see me on the troop train he asked if my parents knew that I was being sent abroad. I said 'No, and we are not allowed off this train until its time for our lot to board the Devonshire.' With that, George got a spare time sheet that he had in his cab 'There you are Harry, write a few lines on this and I'll put it in an envelope and see that your Mother gets it.' About an hour later it was our turn to board the Devonshire, and I went aboard feeling a lot happier because of that chance meeting with George.

The first part of our voyage was quite frightening. Two days out from Liverpool we ran into a terrible storm. The ship did everything but stand on end. There were hundreds of men seasick, dishes flew everywhere and the decks were littered with broken crockery, most of us thought we would never see the Middle East. But as nothing lasts forever, so the awful storm passed and we sailed into calm waters, much to everyone's relief, but we were kept busy the next few days clearing all the decks up and making them presentable again. We were glad to get to the Mediterranean Sea where we could go on deck and enjoy the fresh sea air and sunshine and watch the dolphins follow the ship in the calm blue water. Then after fourteen days, we arrived at our destination, which was Port Said.

We stayed at the transit camp at Port Said for about three weeks to await our postings. When our posting arrived, we had to pack our kit and assemble at the Rail Road. There were about a hundred of us from the Border Regiment and we were told to join the South Lancs Regiment in Jerusalem. The journey was not very pleasant as we were all herded in what appeared to be old wooden cattle trucks and we were a bit scared as we had heard of the rigorous precautions that had to be taken in Palestine against the terrorists. Ginger, myself and a few others were billeted at the Goldsmiths Officers Club which had been taken over by the military. Some of the other lads were sent to the tented camp of D. Company at Damascus Gate. Eventually when we settled in, our duties included 24 hour guards around Jerusalem, including the Governor's House and the King David Hotel. The blitz patrols, which meant house to house searches, and the train escort duties from Palestine to Rafah in Egypt were all quite nerve racking as both Arabs and Jews were hostile towards us. We had to have our rifles attached to our writsts by the rifle sling at all times, even when we went off duty. Even in bed everyone was really wary. Sometimes we only got twelve hours off after 48 hours on. There was only one consolation and that was that the comradeship was great. There was no time for spit and polish parades, but all the troops were still smart and well disciplined throughout the long campaign.

One of the lighter moments that stays bright in my memory was one early morning, after we had been on night patrol and we were returning to the barracks. As we got to Damascus Gate a very rich Arab was coming from one of the villages so we had to ask him to dismount and show his identification. He was very polite and pleasant and his mount was a beautiful grey Arab stallion. The saddle and bridle were heavily embroidered and in the rosy glow of dawn he was a picture to behold. I started to stroke the horse and opened his mouth to get an idea of how old he was. I turned to his owner and said 'Is he about five years old?' He smiled and in perfect English said 'Exactly right. Do you ride?' I said

yes, and with that the Sheik said 'Would you like to try him?' I knew it was against the rules, but the Corporal said 'Go on Woody, but don't go too far out of sight.' I unfastened my rifle and gave it to Ginger to hold for me. I mounted the beautiful grey horse and galloped about 500 yards and then came back. I dismounted and went to shake hands and thank its owner for giving me so much pleasure and the platoon a few moments of relief after an arduous nights patrol. The arab mounted quickly and went off into the distance. Whoever would have dreamt that I, from the back streets of Liverpool, would ride a grey Arab stallion at dawn by Damascus Gate. The memory of it is as bright today, forty years later.

Life in Jerusalem was very hectic with house to house searches and the nightly patrols of the orange and lime groves just outside the city in our search for the many members of the Stern Gang who had committed a lot of atrocities on the British soldiers, who

An Arab stallion similar to the one belonging to the Sheik
which he allowed the author to ride

after all were only carrying out the policies of the British
government. We were not sorry to be relieved of our duties by
the Hampshire Regiment and we moved down to Quastina where
we went back to the strict regimentation of army life, which took
me to many places including Abyssinia, British Somali Land, Port
Sudan and all the various other stations on the Red Sea.

Then one day, our group number was posted up for demob, and
most of the lads I had joined up with, including Ginger, boarded
the old SS Ascanious at Berbera which took us back along the Red
Sea to Port Suez, to await the arrival of the Empire Hallidale which
was to bring us back to Princes Landing Stage at Liverpool, but
unfortunately when we got to Gibraltar I was taken into the sick
bay with malaria, so when we docked at Liverpool I didn't have a
chance to say goodbye to my army pals, as I was taken by

ambulance to the military hospital at Chester, where I had to stay for three weeks until I was sent to York to be demobbed. Within half an hour of reaching York I was on my way back to civilian life with my demob suit and mac, shoes, socks, tie and shirt in a big cardboard box and a travel warrant to Liverpool plus £10. When I got to the station all the spivs recognised the box and followed me offering to buy my demob clothes from me, saying ' £10 for the box soldier' but I just wanted to get on that train that would take me back to Liverpool and home.

Chapter Twelve

Return to Civvy Street

After a couple of weeks at home, adjusting to civilian life again, my father came home one evening and said to me, 'Harry, Mr. Bradley wants you to get in touch with him at Tower Buildings.' Next day about 10.00 am I called in at Tower Buildings. Mr. Bradley welcomed me in and asked me, was I prepared to come back to the Company. When I said I was, he then asked me if I wanted to go to the North End to join the motor vehicles. I said I would prefer to go back to Grafton Street again if it was at all possible. He then said, 'your old pony *Golden Dick* had had an accident and he had to be fired and blistered. He hasn't got any hair on his forelegs and is recuperating in a loose box. If you want to start work with him again, report to Grafton Street on Monday at 7.30 am and I will send the orders through'. So, on that thought, I made my way home, wondering just what the pony looked like. Needless to say, Monday morning wouldn't come quickly enough.

Back in the old routine Dad called me early and we walked to work together. When I got to the stables I was pleasantly surprised to see men who had been prisoners of war, now back doing their jobs. Of course, after two years, some of the old horses that I had known were now replaced by new stock and some of the older men who had been teamsters during the war now found the work too heavy and let the men who had returned take the teams and they were glad just to have one horse. Even Dick Benson had only one horse now but he made sure it was *Velvet*, his old shaft horse, whom he loved.

After giving me a few minutes to talk to the Carters again, after such a long time away, Sam Robinson called me over to the office to welcome me back and tell me what my duties would be. 'I've had word from Mr. Bradley that you are to take *Golden Dick* again I'll take you to see him, he is in the loose box.'

When I saw the pony again my heart sank and a tear came to my eye. He was nothing like the lovely animal I had said goodbye to. Sammy said, 'you must realise Harry, the last six months have been very rough for him. He had his operation and has been out to grass for six months and now he has got to come back to work again. Things are changing fast and the firm is getting mechanised. We had about two hundred horses when you left and we have only got about thirty left now here and about twenty in Cotton Street'.

When I got *Dick* yolked up and ready for the road, my mind went back to the time when I used to show off with this high spirited grey Welsh Cob with all his finery on. Now I felt a bit sad as I headed with him to North West Canning Derry Shed to report to Bill Parry.

Everyone at Coast Lines were glad to welcome me back, saying how tall I had grown but what a horrible job my first load was. A full load of wet hides for Park Lane Station. By the time I got home again, my back muscles were aching with not having done heavy work for such a long time. My mother told me later that two of my mates had called for me at about 8.00 p.m. to go out for the evening but mother told them to call another evening, as I was fast asleep in the chair and she didn't think it was right to awaken me, as I had had a hard first day. But needless to say, after a couple of days I was back in the old routine.

As the months went by *Golden Dick* and I got to be good friends again, I knew that he would never be quite the same, although I got all his gear back to scratch and he was looking flash and all his finery and ribbons on him. The old fire and spirit had gone out of him. All the time I had been in the army he hadn't been fussed over and loved in the way he was used to with me. He was just number 405 to other carters. This was brought home one afternoon when it was almost time to go back to the stables. I put the reins on to drive back to Grafton Street. Gone was the spirit, when I realised that the reins were slack in my hands. To think the way he used to nearly pull my arms out, my heart was heavy for him, wondering what his life had been like while I was away. But you cannot turn the clock back and things have to be accepted.

One evening when I got back to the stables, Sammy the Horsekeeper said, 'Harry, I'm afraid I've got some unpleasant new for you. One of the pony lads needs a pony and *Dick* has got to go to the Cotton Street stables.' My heart sank, although I knew that I couldn't hang on to the pony much longer as there had been a few murmurings about me getting a man's wage now and only having a pony. I had hoped a pony lad from Grafton Street would have been allocated him, then I would have still been able to keep an eye on him and give him a pat when I finished my day's work. However, the bosses at Tower Buildings had told Sammy that *Golden Dick* must go to the North End.

Sammy tried to cheer me up, 'Don't be upset lad, you're getting *Bobbler*'. I couldn't believe my ears. *Bobbler*? he was a huge dark bay with a white blaze down his face who was the pride and joy of a carter named Maurice Austin. I said, 'you can't take *Bobbler* from Maurice'. Sammy laughed, 'I wouldn't like to see anyone take him from Maurice but he is leaving to go to another firm so we thought you were the best lad to take his horse'.

Bobbler was a sight to behold when he had all his lovely bright brasses and gleaming chains on. His coat was like satin and he was thirty hundred weight at least.

When I arrived home that evening to tell Dad all about it. He said, 'Well lad, try not to worry too much about *Golden Dick*. He is not the pony he was before you went into the army and no matter how much you think and worry about him, he will never again be the same as when you first had him'.

My working days with *Bobbler* were quite a shock for him, as he was used to only going to the C.W.S. African Oil Mill, carting cattle food every day to the local rail goods yards, such as Park

Lane, Cheshire Lines or G.W.R. These stations were all close to the mill on the Dock Road, so *Bobbler* was quite used to his daily ration of special horse nuts. No wonder he looked well, as although he would load five tons, it was only short journeys, so he was able to keep his weight.

So, when *Bobbler* and I started our days, it was quite a change for the horse to be going on to the Dock Estate and down the floating roadway and up to town, through all the day to day traffic. But I looked after him as well as I knew how, if only to please Maurice, who had been so dedicated to the horse.

After about six months, a new intake of Irish horses came to the stables, as horse traffic was on the decline and everything was being motorised, good shires were becoming very expensive. Anyway, one day I was told to go and pick up a grey horse called *Tony* and he was to be my horse in future. It seems one of the older carters named Harry Thomas had wanted to have *Bobbler*, and Sammy said that he would have to have him as he had priority over me, he had worked a long time for the Company. So, once again I was taking another horse.

At first I couldn't bring myself to take any great interest in *Tony*, although he was a really good worker who could really move even with a big load on, he had this terrible habit of chewing his forelegs and rubbing his hind legs which made him appear as if he was lousing himself and he got bad tempered and would kick you if you tried to clean him properly. He would not let anyone touch his legs and when he went to be shod he had to be tied down, he got so worked up. So I didn't have the incentive to make him look nice, as it was impossible but you couldn't have had a better horse to work for you.

One day in the middle of winter, after a very heavy fall of snow which had brought a lot of traffic to a halt, five, one horse carters were ordered to Coal Sidings at Cheshire Lines, Brunswick to load bales of stockfish for one of the West Africa boats at North 2 Queens (Palm Line).

As I was one of the last to load and get on our way, I was surprised at the ease at which *Tony* went over the ground. He seemed to glide over the top of the ground, even though there was a raging blizzard but to my amazement when we reached the silo at East Brunswick, the other four horses were bogged down in the snow and couldn't pull their loads but *Tony* tripped his way lightly over the snow to be unloaded at the Palm Line. He certainly earned his oats that day. In the meantime, I went to the mill and borrowed Luke Moran's chain horse and went back to give the other four a 'snatch' that is, a good pull to get them started again.

He was such a willing horse and a good worker, you were never worried to be sent for heavy loads because *Tony* could pull anything and also had the speed which was just the kind of horse companies wanted. But his habit of biting his forelegs grew so bad that his legs were raw and he just could not be touched near his legs and he became impossible to shoe. Eventually, he became so vicious when you tried to touch him that the farriers would not even try to shoe him and although I had tried everything I could to cure him some days he flared up worse than others and even though he was a good worker, a whole day's work would be lost on the days he was taken to a special blacksmith who was noted for dealing with difficult horses.

On many occasions, about six or seven 'one horse' wagons would be sent to Cheshire Lines, Brunswick Station and I would often be working alongside my father and his old mates, so we would all help one another with the loading and discharging. Sometimes there would be forty to fifty railway vans with about one hundred and twenty bales of stockfish in each one. This was Elder Dempsters own work and we would be given a time limit to move them from Brunswick to the Dock Sheds. It was all hand loaded and was hard work, as the bones of the fish would cut your hands. The fish which were for West Africa had been sun and wind dried and baled with wire. The wire would catch the buttons on your jackets and rip your clothes. Besides, it was a smelly job and you dreaded having to get the tramcar home, as people would move away from you.

Another big job was carting large cases of safety matches from 'South One Kings' to the various boats going to West Africa. On many occasions these had to be loaded on to your wagon out of the lofts with double ropes, so one huge case would be hanging over your head while you were busy placing the previous one on your wagon. It was on an occasion such as this that Wally Blackhall, a mate of mine, was loading cartons of matches and I was to be the next one to load. He was half loaded when some cartons which hadn't been slung correctly came out of the sling, knocked him off his wagon and he landed on the ground on his head where he lay unconscious. I managed to calm the horses which had been unsettled by the chaos, then made Wally as comfortable as I could. Then I ran into the avenue to the nearest phone box and dialled 999. The ambulance came quite soon and took him to the Southern Hospital and Wally was off work for about four months. I really missed him, as we did a lot of jobs together; before the accident, he was a very fit lad and before he went into the forces he was quite a good boxer.

As the weeks went by, although *Tony* had my admiration to the way he would work, I was never very happy to have him. No matter how much hard work I put into grooming and seeing to his welfare, he never showed for it, as he couldn't be cured of his awful habit of biting his legs and he got very bad tempered if you tried to put any kind of oils or ointment on, they still irritated him to distraction. So I didn't have any pride when I was with *Tony*. I was so used to a flash pony like *Golden Dick*. All the great big shire horses seemed to be disappearing from the Dock Road and there was no longer any competition amongst carters.

Chapter 13

Dad's Accident

When Wally had been back about six months, we were ordered out to Cheshire Lines at Brunswick Dock Station to cart stockfish to the Palm Line. Tommy Wenham was the first one horse to load up. Then my dad, myself and Wally, in that order. The first two, one horses had made their way to North 2 Queens Dock, leaving Wally and I to follow on. There had been a delay while a ship went through, so the bridge was open. Tommy and Dad had crossed the bridge before it had swung open for the ship leaving us on the other side. When we did get across Tommy had finished lightening his load on the outside hoist where the bales were going up into the loft. The bales had to be slung five at a time in the sling. By the time Wally and I had been in the shed to have our shipping notes passed, my dad had pulled underneath the hoist, ready to be lightened. Tommy was by this time on his way back to Cheshire Lines and my dad had pulled underneath the hoist, ready to be lightened. Half way through discharging his load, the hoistman took the hoist up too quickly, causing the five bales to hit the sill which was jutting out, this caused the sling to burst open and the five big bales to come crashing down on my dad.

The bales knocked him down between the shafts, startling the horse which had started to run but Wally and I managed to grab him by the bridle. After what seemed ages to me but I expect it was only a short space of time, the ambulance arrived to take my dad to hospital but I wasn't allowed to go in the ambulance. I knew that his legs were hurt and I was most upset, but such was the discipline to your work in those days that I had to finish off my father's wagon and then my own with Wally's help of course. He was a staunch friend to me. Then I had to tie dad's horse and wagon behind mine and take the two horses and wagons back to Grafton Street. As it was only just after dinner time, I was given orders to go back to Cheshire Lines. No one from the firm asked what happened. The runner just made a report out that a man had been taken off the job because of an accident.

When I arrived home, my mother had been informed and she had been to see him. She was upset and wanted me to tell her exactly what had happened. Dad was in hospital for about three weeks and had to use two sticks when he came home. Later on he tried to manage with just one walking stick but his right leg never improved and he dragged it behind him.

He never received any money from the firm as a result of this accident, the Carters and Motor Men's Union gave him 10 shillings (50p) a week for six weeks. After that he was only entitled to about 30 shillings (£1.50) a week for him and mother from the sickness and insurance benefit.

My dad never worked again and it broke his heart. He was always waiting for me to tell him the day's new about the men and horses. Now and again the men at our depot would club up a few shillings and say to me, 'Give your dad that for a pint'. It would be about a pound or twenty five shillings but they couldn't do it too often, as other carters would be ill or off work with some trouble or other and they tried to collect a bob (5p) off each man to give the sick man something. I used to put a few shillings extra of my own to make it seem as though the men at work had given more generously, which of course they couldn't, as they were poorly paid and most of them had large families to cater for. Dad would want to know how everyone was. 'Tell them I'll be back before they know it' he would say. But as the months went by, I knew somehow that dad would never be a carter again.

One or two old pals would call up at the house after they had been home and had had their evening meal and if they had a few shillings extra from a bit of overtime they would take dad for a pint or two to the local. But dad was very proud and wouldn't go unless he could buy a round in return. Beer was 5d (2½p) a pint so if I managed to slip him half a crown (12½p), I knew he could buy his round and a few Woodbines into the bargain.

About fifteen months after the accident it was dad's birthday on the Saturday and I had seen a flash tie that I knew he would like and promised to get it if he would wear it that night when the whole family were taking him out to the local pub. He told everyone to go ahead and save some seats. For some reason he wanted to just walk the distance to the pub with me. He talked away and was in good spirits all evening and as public houses closed at 10.00 p.m. in those days, we were all home and having a bit of supper, which Mother got for us all by about 10.30 p.m. We all said what a happy evening we had all enjoyed and we got to bed about 12.30 a.m.

At about 4.00 a.m. I was woken by noises and running around. My brother's bed was empty so I got up, wondering what was the matter. It seemed that my dad had called out my mother's name very loudly and then collapsed and died. We just couldn't believe it as he had seemed in such good spirits all evening. The whole family were in a state of shock.

As it happened, it was my Sunday turn out and I had to go and feed and water all the horses, otherwise they would be stamping around the stalls, waiting for their food and water. So, heartsick as I was, I knew I must go. On my way, I met another carter. He knew by my face that something was wrong and when I told him he said, 'you make your way home lad, I'll do your Sunday turn and report what has happened in the morning'. I thanked him and was relieved that I wouldn't have to worry about work.

After Dad's funeral, life had to be resumed as best as possible but the life had gone out of me and I felt as weak as a kitten. To say that Wally Blackhall did his own work and half of mine is an understatement he literally did both our jobs and never once did he utter one word of complaint or tell me to pull myself together. He knew how much it hurt me to pass the stall with my dad's horse in it.

After dad's death, the company sent his horse to Cotton Street, and it was given to a carter named Teddy Hatch. About a couple of weeks after, I saw Teddy with a different horse. 'Where is *Barney*?' I asked him. He said, 'Harry, you won't believe this but I only had him a couple of days and when I came in one morning he was dead in the stall'. This of course added to my misery I couldn't eat and I didn't want company. All my old mates left me alone, knowing that I would come round in my own good time, although it took over six months for me to start feeling normal again. It was hard for me, as I could imagine my dad when I was going along the Dock Road, giving me a shout and a wave as we did our jobs and asking each other 'where are you assigned today?' and if it was a rotten job, pulling each other's legs about it, or finding him an extra dry sack to put over him if it had been a wet day.

The thing that finally made me realise that I must leave this job to gain peace of mind was when I heard that *Golden Dick* had died. Tommy Wenham told me that the horse had died of a broken heart. He had been so well loved at Grafton Street but at Cotton Street he was just another pony.

The days and weeks seemed to drag by and I still had no will left to get interested in my work again the memory of my father was everywhere.

Then, one evening, I just said to my mother when we were alone for a few minutes, 'Mum, I think I will have to leave the cartage company as it's too heartbreaking being reminded of dad every day'. 'Well son', she said, 'I don't blame you as I know it's hard. You did everything with your dad and you must miss just having breakfast and walking to work with him. If you cannot bear it anymore, give in your notice. You will get a job anywhere as I know what a hard worker you are. Your dad used to tell me that, so do what you think is the best'.

When I went to work the next day I told Wally about my decision to leave. He said, 'Well Harry,. I'm glad you have told me as I have been wanting to look for a better job myself. Now that I am married the money is too low for us to manage but I didn't want to leave while you needed a helping hand. We will give our week's notice in together'. If ever a fellow had a friend in need, I had found it in Wally.

When word got around that I would be leaving, Luke Moran, always a good friend, asked me if he could have my rubber tyred truck. Teddy Bainbridge asked for my long driving reins but all my own brasses and finery that I used to put on *Golden Dick* I couldn't part with as they held too many precious memories, so I took them home and wrapped them up and put them into my dad's saddlery chest, never to be used again.

When Friday evening came and we had said our goodbyes, Wally and I walked up to the Flat Iron public house in the middle of Mill Street. We had a farewell pint together and a talk of times past and I must admit my eyes were moist as we said goodbye. I knew without doubt I would never have such a good working pal like Wally and I still think of him with great affection.

So ended my days as a carter and now, if my footsteps return to the Dock Road, it saddens me to think that it was once teeming with traffic, men, great horses, steam engines, ships in the docks and the train on the overhead railway. There isn't even one small plaque anywhere in memory of all the hard work, sweat and pain suffered by both men and the great heavy horses to even show we had passed that way.

We might never have existed there is nothing at all to remember us by.

(Editor's note:)
With the possible exception of this book.

Glossary

Carters

Liverpool Corporation

T. Jones	W. Tyrer	M. Elberg	G. Johnston	T. Lovat
A. Brookes	G. Dowler	J. Swift	F. Cross	G. Clinton
J. Goodier	F. Shaw	W. Fairhurst	R. Kelly	A. Fletcher
J. Roberts	W. Hall	F. Boswell	G. Wooding	D. Socket

M Mosley (Mouse)   W. Holden. (later to be Lord Mayors Coachman)
T. Taylor (day cook for horses)   S. Gaskell (night cook for horses)

Liverpool Cartage

J. Thornton	R. Sinclair	R. Benson	G. Sinclair	H. Thomas	J Baxendale
F. Pizzar	W. Woods	M. Austin	L. Moran	J. Hammond	J. Swift
E. Hughes	T. Mather	J. Hunter	C. Taylor	T. Baimbridge	W. Blackhall
L. Furlong	J. Dowd	J. Baxendale	G. Wooding	H. Wooding	

J. Ainsworth (Woodbine Willy)   T Hatch (I of Bacon)   G Moran (Reverend)
T Swift (Deaf)   T Whenham (The bully)   E Horton (Popeye)

Firms

Jarvis Robinson	David Jones	William Harper	James Foley	David Rees
William Lucy	Josp Knall	George Tulloch	G.B. Edwards	C.W.H. Taylor
J.C. Halsall	Morris Jones	Arthur Hughes	Larry Marr	P & T Fitzpatrick
Hobbs Clarke	J. Fielding	A.V. Crutchley	Mark Reville	J.W. Walker
M.A. Keenan	Richard Proctor	Joseph Heap	Cranmer Cartage	Liverpool Cartage

Union Road Cartage Suttons Carriers George Davies (Steamers)

Steam Engines

George Davies   Kirkdale Haulage   W. Lewis Haulage

Carriers

Carter Paterson	Bouts Tillotson	Allied Freight	Thomas Orford	L. M. S.
I.O.M. Steam Packet		L.N.E.R.	C.L.C.	G. W. R.

Elder Dempster Lines Limited

Accra Mail Boat	Appapa Mail Boat	Princes landing stage and Canada Dock
Deido West Africa	South-west Brunswick	
Fulani West Africa	Harrington West Toxteth	
Tamele West Africa	Tarkwa West Africa	Two Heavy Lifting boats
Sanslu West Africa	Swedru West Africa	Fulani West Africa
Quay Foreman	Phil Harpers	
Wharfingers	George Lee	Harold Pimlett Jack Greenwood

Mary Kingsley West Africa David Livingstone   Sobo West Africa Sherboro West Africa
Onishita ex Paddy Henderson Line   Capt. Thomas
Calabar   Small passenger vessel based mostly on the West Coast of Africa,
         brought back to Liverpool to be sold.

Palm Line   North 2 Queens

Benin Palm Ashanti Palm   Takoradi Palm   Lagos Palm
Wharfingers   Cyril Maud Stan Maud

Booker Line

Harrington Dock
Amerkura & Arakaka   Georgetown   Demerara

Booth Line North 1 Kings
South America   Hilary
Brazil nuts in bulk discharged in baskets weighed on quay.

Harrison Line
East Brunswick Dock   Load Liverpool by the grain silo discharge Birkenhead
All boats named after occupations:
Herdsman   Vera Cruz   Geologist   Caracas Astrologer   Mexico

Sir Alfred Reid   All Coast Lines
West Canning   East Victoria   E. Trafalgar   West Trafalgar   N.S.E. Nelson
W. Bramley Moore   Ulster Monarch   Ulster Prince
Named after coasts: Antrim Coast   Killarney   B.I.S.P. Cold   Leinster Munster
East Princes   West Princes   Johnney Ellison,
Quay Foremen   George Wilson,   Bert Flaughty

John Holt Line
N.E. Brunswick   Alfred Holt   Jonathon Holt
Wharfinger   Jim Lloyd
C.W.S. African Oil Mill   Elder Dempster Sailmakers Department
Dominion Tea Co Ltd   James Laver Stamps and Books   Calwell A.S.B.,
Burmyeat Dalzell & Nicholson Shipchandlers   Porters Flag Makers, Kings Dock Mill
McSymonds Ship Stores   Crescent Printing   Standard Brands, Benn' Gardens

Horses
Albert	Bluebottle	Barn Owl	Caxton	Charlie
Cormarant	CarbonDuchess	Camp Bed	Daredevil	Delightful 153
Darkie 189	Demon	Emblem 181	Elixer	Exeter
Expert 420	Freddie	Final Shot	Hilda 163	Homer 152
Imperial 168	Improver 180	Indigo 144	Iceberg	Inkspot
John Bull	Idol119	Indus 191	West	Jubilee
Kit Kat (Mr Lees pony Jackie)		Kipper Kelly (sold to West Derby Sewerage Farm)		
Kaffier 160	Karl 135	Kinsman	Kingfisher	Opal
Zell	Zoo			

Mail Ponies   Harty   Izadaw   Jet   Joe
Lord Mayors Horses   Coachman Mr Oldfield (Son Brian)
Cork   Jimmy   Sydney   Michael
Groom Mr Smith   Rolls Royce AKA 1

East Princes Checkers
Wharfinger   Johnny Ellison   Jack Copple
          Mr Faye   Mr Shaw

West Princes Checkers   Tommy James   E. Connor   B. Wilkes   E. Molyneux
G. Wilson   Foreman   Express Shed
Bert Flaughty   Quay Foreman

Scruttons of London Stevedores Men in charge at B. SSGO Ltd
Mr Hunter   Mr Curtis   Mr Newman   Mr Robinson
Two special and helpful crane drivers at Scruttons were:
George Judge (Runabout)   Matty (Heavy crane)
Steam cranes permanent express shed   Steam cranes permanent blitz shed
Heavy lifting crane for deck cargo   Permanent Princes half tide.
EDL cranes mostly runabout rapiers plus quite a few electric cable cranes.
Battery boxes of various colours in sheds sometimes had to be towed into position by
horses or an electric Bogey.

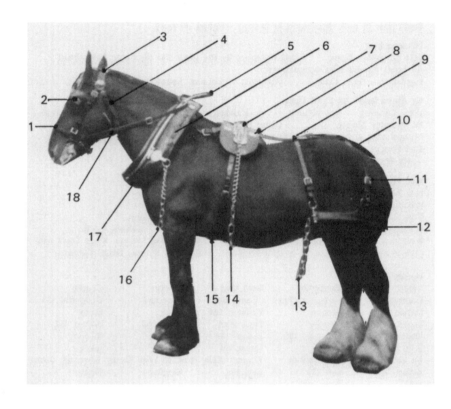

1	Nose Band	10	Loinstraps
2	Blinkers	11	Loinstraps
3	Bridle	12	Breeching
4	Throat Lash	13	Breeching Chains
5	Topping Strap	14	Ridgeworth Chain
6	Hames or Jambles	15	Girth Strap
7	Crank	16	Shoulder Chains
8	Saddle	17	Collar
9	Crupper	18	Bearing Rein

Bearing Rein The means by which the horse is directed by carter

Blinkers: Leather flap fitted to each side of head at eye level to prevent the horse from seeing sideways.

Breechings: A broad thick band of leather which is held in a horizontal position around the horses buttocks by the loinstraps. The Breeching has at each end a metal link attached to a length of chain (Breechings chain) which is fixed to the shafts of the waggon allowing the horse to exert pressure when leaning back into the Breeching to reverse the waggon.

Bridle: The apparatus around the head by which the horse is checked or restrained.

Collar: Made of leather usually stuffed with straw. Collars were very often made especially for the individual horse to suit its neck proportions enabling the collar to sit comfortably in place.

Crank: Steel bridge placed across saddle to allow the Ridgeworth chain to rest over the horses back and hang on either side. Each end of the chain is fixed to the waggons shafts to carry their weight.

Crupper: Strap of leather fastened at one end to the saddle and passing along the horsers back and under the tail; used to keep the saddle in its place.

Girth Strap: Leather strap girdled around the horses belly and attached at each end to the saddle to hold it in position.

Hames: The two bow shaped steel bars one on each side of a draught horses collar.

Loinstraps: Leather straps which hang over the horses rear flanks attached to the Crupper at the top and are adjustable to allow the Breechings to hang at the desired level.

Nose band: A leather strap around the lower part of the horses head just above the mouth joined on to the Bridle which holds it in position.

Saddle: A padded leather band in some respects similar to a riding saddle but much smaller and lighter in weight. This rests over the horses back and is held in position with the Girth strap.

Shoulder chain: A chain fixed to both the Collar and the waggon shafts which allows the horse to pull the waggon.

Throat lash: Leather strap attached to the head of the Bridle at each side to hold it in position.

Topping or Hames strap: Strap across the two Hames bars and which can be tightened bringing the bars closer together at the top.

References:

1 **Brights** Polished galvanised chains and brasses used mainly for Shows and fine days to enhance the horses beauty.
2 **Blacks or Gears** The same equipment as Brights but black and varnished, used for everyday work.
3 **Pikle or Pitch fork** Long handled fork with 2 prongs used for lifting, pitching and turning hay or straw.
4 **Olley** Smooth stone pebble placed inside kettle which rattled when water boiled, also stopped furring.
5 **Soft Soap** A jelly usually dark brown in colour sold by weight not to be confused with "Aunt Sally" disinfectant.
6 **Duraglit** Cotton wadding impregnated with polishing agent used for cleaning brasses the same as Brasso.
7 **Bridle** Leather headgear used to control and steer horse.
8 **Hames or Jumbles** Equipment which fitted on to horses collar and attached to shoulder chains enabling horse to pull wagon.
9 **Necking strap** Long leather strap used to hold Hames on to collar assisted by Topping strap and Drawdown strap to secure the hames around collar on horses neck.
10 **Leather saddle** Attached by strap on each side of collar fastened by two buckles.
11 **Girth strap** Leather belt attached to each side of saddle and tightened under horses belly to hold saddle in position.
12 **Crank** Metal fixture which fits into the Tree of Saddle.
13 **Ridgeworth chain** Chain which fits over the crank and is attached at each end to the shafts enabling them to be lifted to desired height.
14 **Crupper** Attached to rear of saddle and running down centre of horses back enabling two loin straps to be fixed to the Breeching which goes around the horses rear used when reversing the wagon.
15 **Boston** Small fence or barrier used to separate horses that are in stalls inside stables.
16 **Breeching** Wide strap around horses buttocks allowing horse to lean back and act as a brake for the cart.
17 **Collar** Oval shaped leather collar around horses neck (see page 110) for further detail.
18 **Brasso** Liquid abrasive cleaning material
19 **Dolly Bag** A muslin bag containing Blue Dye used to enhace the whiteness during washing.
20 **Brake** Solid wooden block covered with leather which pressed againsr wheels to restrain cart whilst in motion, applied by driver pulling on a pole, or pressing a foot pedal
21 **Pole Wagon** Exercise wagon, with a single pole in place of the shafts with a horse on either side of the pole.
22 **Dandy Brush** Oval shaped brush used for grooming horses tail and mane.
23 **Aunt Sally** Liquid Soap product partialy geletanous.
24 **Curry Comb** Steel comb used for cleaning horse brushes.
25 **Brasses** Decorative Brass ornaments attached to leather straps.
26 **Face Pieces** Decoration for horses forehead.
27 **Loin Straps** Straps that fit across loins to secure Crupper and Breeching straps (see detail on page110).
28 **Martindales** Decorative piece of harness which hangs in front of horses front legs containg brasses.